<u>Coming Home with Gratitude</u>

Namaste.

I am a teacher, mother, lover, traveller, searcher, designer, hatha yoga & meditation teacher, women's intuitive lifestyle coach & expressive, living words writer.

A few years ago, after the passing of my dear father, I experienced a deep, spiritual understanding of life that changed everything for me. This beautifully profound transformational experience, is the basis of everything that I teach and write about today. It is the foundation of how I help women come to understand and value, unwanted body-mind behaviours.

I hope my story inspires you to see the truth about yourself, that you are just as happy, confident and peaceful as you were when you were a little kid. More so, that old patterns and conditioning will begin to change and shift for you too.

There is nothing like the present moment to re-learn to re-love the self. Carpe diem!

Thankyou,

Sarah Duff

Are we our soul, body
and mind or not ?!
Some intrestiny life experience
of your double from up North...
Thank you for being my
next GURU
love Pattyca xxx

Coming Home with Gratitude

Learn more at http://www.sarahduff.co.uk

Email: sarah@sarahduff.co.uk

This book is dedicated to you dear reader. Here's to your truth.

My deepest gratitude goes to the many people I've encountered along the way, to experience this deep spiritual understanding of life that changed everything for me, a full 360 degrees' turnaround.

Coming Home with Gratitude describes real people and a series of chronological, personal, life changing events, shared from the core of a normal, northern girls heart.

Family and friends would suggest that the majority of this account is 20 % exaggerated because Sarah just loves to make anecdotes more interesting!

To maintain the narrative, time has been condensed to bracket a 12-month period. Also, personal names have been changed to protect true identities. However, may this written version do them honorable justice and also offer the reader new ways to live in love and light with boundless joy, the very essence of our human nature.

What is time, my son persistently enquired as a youngster?
Sarah could never fully respond with an appropriate answer. Until now, that is, in this mature body, which can express a truer proposal: that one senses that 'it' doesn't necessarily exist, that it spontaneously combusts, that it is a static presence, that it is a human creation, beautiful, yet very necessary illusion; or that it is one's perspective on simultaneous levels of awareness.

Contents

He was lame
As a 3 legged dog
Screamed as he came
Through the fog
If you are the light
Give me a light Buddy

Leonard Cohen 1965

Love and light dear ones.

Introduction

Who am I? Where am I from? The vital life force energy that created my very being where did that come from? As far back as I can remember I have struggled, questioned and wanted a resolution for these existential sentiments, or my 'mind' or something within the depth of my core did. But then again, I always thought that I was just a bit weird, possessing different thought processes from everybody else, away from the mainstream. So, I buried this deep within my being and lived asleep, but unknowingly still blessed at the same time, as we all are. Life for Sarah went on.

Without expectation, a powerful, intense awakening to 'something' different within me arose during the passing of my beautiful father.
And so my quest began. A quest for answers, for a solution, for words, meanings, and most importantly, for understanding and inquiry of self. Books, internet, journals and television documentaries all kept my left brain logical side relatively seduced. Yet the cheekier Monkey Mind questioned, the more Monkey Mind wanted expansion. Tenfold. Until finally, Monkey Mind could take no more and whispered, "Let go, let's go."

Both tentatively and reassuringly, he enveloped my hand in his firm grip and we headed off into the unknown, holding so much gratitude in our full and heavy hearts.
My family didn't know what to make of this newfound assertiveness, guessing a mid-life crisis or mental breakdown or such like.
Thankfully, they graciously left me to it and I literally just walked out the door. Classic case of crazy meltdown or what? However, rationally, my kids were young adults with their own agenda, belonging to life rather than to me now; and the husband, devoted to his work and his service to the construction industry, was more than happy to be left in his own little bubble.
No excuse needed. This was it, time for Sarah's spiritual growth and with her accomplice in tow, good old friend Monkey Mind. What a beautifully scary coupling. What an oxymoron.

Feed the little bugger, keep him sweet, keep him fed and watered, that oh so sweet and charming Monkey Mind of mine. And I did, gaining many a wonderful insight from direct experiences in nature and from many beautiful places including Europe, Asia, the heart of England, the Middle East and rugged Scotland.

It was over there in Dubai that my 12-month journey home finally exhausted itself. Rather like Forest Gump's realization that he should simply give up running, I too just stopped dead in my tracks. Well that, and being physically ill and confined to bed with a serious bout of Dengue fever (a severe form of Malaria) that completely poleaxed me, forcing me to sweat 'it' out even deeper and contemplate my existence even further in the very dark shadows of my being.

Fortunately, like the rising of our glorious sunshine, after 6 long, tedious days and a temporary paralysis of mind on the apartment rooftop, my higher-self kindly picked me up and dusted me down. Then followed, like an obedient puppy, the karmic housekeeping.

Befriending Monkey Mind

WOAHHH… the ever advancing 21st century technology maintains Monkey Mind in a constant state of flux; electromagnetically charged chaotic entertainment, immersed in supercharged quantum vibrational orbit and ever chattering away mindlessly like an amphetamine junkie.   Apps, social media, blogging, internet shopping, YouTube, iPods, iPads, irons, only kidding on that one. Although the cordless, base plates types are pretty impressive to say the least. However, I am an old fashioned or maybe just a lazy girl at heart, whichever way you want to look at it. My dry, clean jeans are placed under my bed mattress to get rid of the creases. And for more delicate items? I swear by extra fabric conditioner for crease free, fragrant clothes. Although some friends claim that this technique loses the 'bant' in the fabric and clogs up the washer? Horses for courses, I say.

Yep, this digital age we live in is very impressive. Anything and everything is available online, next day delivery, online, no problem. No wonder Monkey Mind is heavily sedated, to the point of intoxication, by a woozy, toxic cocktail, ready and available for another hit. Yet another intoxicating, energy-consuming, keep that Monkey Mind sedated hit. Buy that new device, upgrade, up-cycle, expand yourself through the material world. Feed that pain, feel that fear. Happy days.
What's this, another influx of refugees? Further destruction? An uncovering of yet more celebrity paedophiles? Banks collapsing? Fat corporate company cats, sniffing cocaine fear? How can they keep satisfied any longer their, so far, loyal co-dependent workers and create for them healthier paychecks and fatter lifestyles?

I felt this constant daily influx of stimulation, keeping our very being away from the absolute truth, though Monkey Mind enjoys a great vacation in the process.
In essence, all is not well on our beloved Mother Earth. Not only in terms of its very structure and energetic dynamics but in many other ways too: the prescribed 'news channel' feeds us a never-ending worldwide cycle of 'catastrophes' that occur, the increasing floods and the climate shift. Oh dear.

Life is speaking to all humanity, screaming out loud to 'wake up', to love and express compassion for all of humankind. A new beginning is paramount. Smell the coffee! Look too, at the infrastructure, at the healthcare system, Education, local authorities and communities, each and every aspect. Whether within the private or public sector, each faculty is suffering, over stretched and manipulated, like a washed up mangled love affair, not only in reference to other beings but to our Mother Earth, too.

Ask you're being this question? How can we live in a society in the 21st Century that glorifies, celebrates and even praises warfare, destruction, killing and shooting? Turn on the TV, open a newspaper, it's there. Soak it up and absorb. At the same time all this hides love, making love, giving, sharing, expressing love? Why are we so conditioned to hide our very essence? Our very being? Our very nature? The one we are so innocently born with, until conditioning teaches us to put some clothes on and cover up! Why, Monkey Mind? Why?

Please excuse my/our inability to write/select/choose the 'correct' expression in some of my writing throughout this unfolding of my spiritual journey thus far. Sarah and her friend have an issue with selecting the appropriate word or concept at times, especially during the flow of writing, whether it be reading, re-reading, comprehending, internalizing or scanning. You see it is a constant state of change for me, him, her, it, who is even thinking that? LOL.

But Sarah will not apologize for this seeming lack of clarity and empathy for the reader. On the contrary, in truthfulness, how can one ever express what we feel and experience with words alone? Often, subtle silence or a picture cues information, gives us all the clues we need and speak volumes if we are deeply enough aware to pay attention. When does one ever have the time to really ponder within a sacred silence? Does life ever give you space to do just that, to be still? Or is that something that does not resonate with you? Do you like being totally surrounded by people to keep you entertained? Does quiet time alone make you feel friendless, lonely, isolated?

As a mother, professional, housewife, teacher, accountant, lover, cook, administrator, taxi driver, fashion advisor, nurse, good cop, bad cop, to name but a few character costumes that I have worn/wear - struggling even to find a little alone 'me' time - did I ever manage to really stop, be quiet and simply Be?

Also, in that professional role as a teacher, Sarah was subjected to that programme of study where educators are conditioned to the fundamental principle of using and applying age appropriate terminology to young children in the form of those very concepts she was questioning; that they are paramount for growth? Yet, once I'd stepped onto the path of the 'awakening,' boy how that traditional beast was taken down.

Initially, this was very difficult to do, to come away from fully; it often still is, but I find it similar to unravelling an old, heavy, knit woolen jumper. It's a lengthy process. For some reason, I am inclined to suggest that these concepts/words/labels can be quite damaging for children, as they harness natural God given creativity, which certainly has impact and further implications into adulthood as those ideals are formulated and set in stone.

As a human race, we have never been taught the idea of 'letting go,' or that it is even safe to do that. Not in 3D existence anyway, most certainly not, little cheeky Monkey Mind you.

My present body is female yet I will refer to my 'Monkey Mind' as male. This is what he feels like to me. Stereotypically, he has male features, a hairy masculine torso and very strong, well-defined, enveloping hands. Yes, hands are a big thing of mine. Sarah is a very visual learner. She just loves imagery! Do feel free to create your own 'Build A Bear' mind monkey version for our own gratification. 'It' can even wear a bathing or space suit if you like! Absolutely no rules, no right or wrong way. In fact, what is up, what is down? Or even left or right, for that matter? Do these words/concepts even exist coherently in this illusionary existence called life? Do they even make sense or have clarity?

As adults and teachers, how can we demand that children fully understand these misconceptions without allowing them to challenge and investigate their very nature? Ever tried explaining to a child how to paint a green house, let alone a class of 30 primary aged children? Hilariously fascinating.

A funny, shared fact is that good teachers have too much to learn and remember and know this deep in their hearts. In fact, we all do. We know absolutely nothing. As a collective 'they' don't and can't remember all of the curricular learning objectives as set out by the ever changing statutory national curriculum. Many, speaking from experience, know that there are just too many facts to appreciate. If this is the case for adults, how must a young and growing, expanding, vibrant being feel in relation to self, being expected to retrieve taught information at the drop of a hat? Where is this information stored? Long or short term memory? Is it felt, even?

Equally, is the young self deemed inferior in light of this rapid response environment that adult beings are cultivating? Sarah remembers as a kid feeling 'thick' at Math, nothing/no one helping her to resonate with it. Yet as an adult educator, her love of creative mathematical approaches was embraced by kids who just couldn't get enough and would whizz through math challenges and ask for more. Who wouldn't love playing with a beach ball to learn the times tables? Tut, tut, tut, not in this paradigm.

Without deeper sensory experience, without the joy of experiencing 'it' through the senses, how can we expect them to learn 'it' from an A4 white paper sheet; which in turn, produces a standardized government approved judgment: at age related expectations or below. How destructive!

Sarah feels (or who? Not sure) that within the education system especially, it so damaging to enforce such a belief system on such young, tender, conscious-expanding beings; and that these limitations actually undervalue and undermine self-worth and potential creativity. This is especially true during the most precious time of a child's life, the downloading period, at 7-10 years old; when learning and objectivity is grasped from the outer body through many sources and drawn within to set the precedence for conditioning, values or beliefs, or all three, whichever way you choose to look at it?

Parents are expected to fully place their trust and judgment in the educators of today; it has been instilled and conditioned in them to, lol. How very ironic when you think of some of the beings we have trusted with the care of our special little ones and who have so abused this trust. Yet the cycle continues. Incredible.

Every child is special, unique, and has the potential for any super power they so naturally desire: mathematician, writer, scientist, footballer, brain surgeon, geologist etc., etc. You get the jist. Yet are parents foolishly blindfolded into believing that this deep, enriching, widening, government-approved curricular learning will guarantee their special one a special future space in existence?

What are we allowing our children to be set up for? A star protégé – born from them-projected out into the life, destined for a grandiose lifestyle, enriched by plentiful nouns in every capacity?

You want a Range Rover, corporate dinner lunches, matching Rolexes, luxury holidays, FT Index shares, detached stone, state-of-the-art home, season-tickets in a private booth, children in boarding school, glamorous Italian designer label wearing 'beautiful' other half? You can have it all. Can you sense how delicious this all sounds in the eyes of the delicate? What image are we portraying to our generations to follow? That material wealth has become our very being, our very essence and our very nature. How have we come to live in a world that places value on heavily saturated, Westernized ideals? How Monkey Mind, my friend? How? Rant over.

Deep in my core level, on the subject of education, I had always felt more inclined to cross the bridge over to the new age verge, yet simultaneously felt drawn to the benefits of the mainstream principles too. Thus, I often hovered on middle ground to find a balance.   Damn my indecisive, air head, Libra tendencies sometimes!

The Passing of 'Pop'

Sarah cannot remember for sure, the time, the place, or even the sensory memory as to when she felt the world was back to front, upside down or the wrong way round. Or any other way one fancies to look at it.

However, she can clearly recall the deeply moving passing of her Father and the questions that started to arise from the subconscious to the conscious level, the self -enquiring mind. Sarah developed a feeling of knowing that something felt very different inside to what she had felt before. She experienced a 'calling' to something far greater than her, but what? Sarah was going to find out, she has a curious personality.

I have often pondered the direction of my journey so far, particularly during quiet contemplation or meditation practice which, simply put, is where I find that solace, that still place within my being. That perfectly, unmoving clear blue sky, which signifies that all is well, all is perfect and always has been (for each and every being also!)

This was a massive realization for me, like the highest rush of adrenalin imaginable, similar to being catapulted off The Big One rollercoaster ride at Blackpool Pleasure Beach, into the Cosmos, 'To infinity and beyond,' as Buzz Lightyear would sing. Intense, eh?

I never envisaged that something so profound stirred within me, something that would literally take hold of my life and make me fully reassess my belief systems which I had thought, up to a point, to be true.

At the beginning of my journey, I did not fully understand the implications; or that this internal hungry desire would be unleashed, like a pack of hungry wolves knocking on your door at one in the morning when all you want to do is sleep but they will not go away. Understand this metaphor, the wolves just would not leave, no matter how many cigarettes I gave them to smoke or alcoholic drinks to drown in. They persisted howling at the door.

Yes, beautiful, beloved father, the passing of your body, even at such a dark and heart wrenching time of year, you managed to shed so much light. (Christmas is never a good time for our family.)

Unbelievably, within that short week's timeframe, you managed to share so much beautiful, abundant grace and love and an ultimate gift from life, through your subtle bodily teaching, your vibrational heart. What a very special Christmas gift that you gave to us all! Thank you.

It's only very recently that I've come to be able to fully articulate the message you conveyed, even though I felt a jarring of sorts at the time and witnessed something very profound. No words can express my deep gratitude to you, nor my unconditional love for everything you ever shared with us all, such valuable lessons.

Dad, I don't know how you managed to constantly reflect my shining light within, on a daily basis. Yes, Sarah is a greedy girl and a demanding creature who truly misses that.

Until I started my adventure on this path, I did not understand the concept of beings as mirrors for each other; your perception of me is a reflection of you and all that. Sarah not only speaks for herself but for the rest of the crazy, beautiful clan also.

Isn't everyone's family crazily beautiful also, crazily perfect, exactly how we are supposed to be, at precisely the right time? Wearing the appropriate masks, in service to others for growth and expansion?

Only recently, have I been able to summate into words what I actually witnessed and observed through your physical, bodily passing Dad. After watching Dr. Wayne Dyers film, The Shift; something in me immediately clicked into place and 'it' registered. I experienced that wonderful AHA light bulb, brain alerting moment when Dr. Dyer discusses dying and uses magical words to deliver this statement: '*Don't leave your body with the magic still inside.*'

This very sentiment Dad, you subtly communicated through to us all, despite the heart monitors, intravenous drips and other medical equipment your body was hooked up to to keep your major organs open and breathing, to ease your pain and earthly discomfort.

How I felt and shared that with you, how Ram Dass is so right in sharing,

'*In the presence of death is grace, within two levels of awareness.*'

So true. On the one hand death is a loss, sadness, shattering and on another level it is a blessing, a relief, a joy from pain.

All I know is to feel, on a deeper level, this; through the Divine, Consciousness, Essence, God, Allah, Buddha, Jesus Christ, Christ Consciousness, call it what you will, in your next body, Dad, you will live your magic. That vintage sports car will be waiting for you on your driveway, for a leisurely Sunday afternoon spin because you can. Will you be wearing your Gizmo, furry hat and fingerless leather gloves? Why, of course! Feel that you will also conquer Kilimanjaro, as you discussed, at least to base camp. So I will see you there, beautiful, very beautiful soul.

Yes, teacher's prerogative, always going off on a tangent. So, drawing back to my original statement/question, when did Sarah wake up? Was there significance in time? Or was it a mere collection of experiences and opportunities that so gloriously guided my very being, to be sat here in my gorgeous friend's home, channeling this writing, pen in hand, with Merlin's Magic-the Heart of Reiki playing softly in the background and the very impressive willow tree in the garden, softly dancing to the tunes of my keyboard, swaying and singing, all is one, all is energetically one. Whilst simultaneously, observing the branches as they rise and fall, gracefully in melodic flow, that encourages my fingers to stream these letters down onto the keyboard.
But who is writing? Sarah? Consciousness? Monkey Mind? Let's see.

The Journey

Life, universe or cosmos, whichever term resonates with you, when you open up to it, is the most **magical** place ever!! This is very true, beings. Why yes, of course it is easy for me to say this but let me share my experiences with you, to help you feel it. In the true words of Ray Mears, and Confucius (around 450 BC) and probably repeated by many other significant beings also:

'Tell me and I will forget, show me and I may remember, involve me and I will understand.'

My intention as I write? To involve you in this wonderful, streamed account of experiential learning. The optimal kind for the body's intelligence.

Some of you may 'wake up' to your own joy, blessed to evolve your vehicle of consciousness with your very own intimate, humbling, magical expression of human experience. Some of you may not.

Yogi Bhajan, 1976, once stated, as shared by another very beautiful yogi master who I was universally fortunate to meet during my travels in the very empowering holy city of Rishikesh:

'We are all a random slice of spirit, having a random human, biological experience.' Om shanti, shanti, shanti.

From experience, I can only suggest, it is like slowly peeling the outer layers of an onion, one by one, (visual cue prompt). Awakening often feels like that. Peeling one's outer layers off, realizing one's shit, realizing the need to dump that shit into the wild forest, just as wild animals do.

Do the small rabbits, foxes or deer ask permission to dump their shit on Mother Earth? No, she is in abundance, let go. Nature speaks volumes and when we connect with it we have access to all the answers we ever need. Nature, God, God, Nature, same difference. Mucho amigos en la naturaleza!

Okay, now that is a really good teacher opening statement, I love it; I can just imagine the look on my former head teacher's face on that one! LOL! Love you really.

Anyway, there is a minefield of self -help books to point and guide an enquiring mind along the way. A good tip, just use your inner guidance system to allow in whatever resonates with you alone. We are all unique individuals, yet one source, merely peeking out with different sets of eyes.

Therefore, (much better opener here, old level 3B National Curriculum I think) go slowly, go very slowly, a forest does not say, 'Hurry up trees grow taller,' nor does it shout at the flowers for not being colorful enough, or for not shining brightly enough.
'Hey you bush over there, you're way too bushy, get a trim, you're uncontrollable!' Blimey, no. All in good time, no haste.... observe patiently, everything unfolds perfectly so and in full accordance with the law of life.
Nor does the sun say, 'Hey I'm only shining on the lushest flowers today; I'm going to ignore the weeds.' The sun simply and perfectly shines and radiates that pure loving energy on everything.
We share/are this universal, life force energy; let this be your daily mantra.
Observe, witness, with no praise or judgment. Let it be and then let it go. We are all returning home, travelling different yet necessary paths and encountering different experiences along the way.

Self-help spiritual books can be of use but can get mind boggling, especially concerning such expressions as; Kundalini, Shakti Kundalini, ascension, enlightenment, DNA cellular reconstruction, energy, twin flames, channeling higher self, source energy and vortex. Yip, a whole new language to be soaked up and absorbed.
From experience.... simplicity is key. Does the monkey in the mind need to know? Who is even asking this question? From an analytical left brain point of view, something far bigger, far greater than the body alone.
Let me share my story with you of 'Coming Home with Gratitude.'
Sarah hopes that you will enjoy the dialogue from my big, fat, juicy open spiritual heart and that somewhere deep within, it may light a spark and resonate with you also?
If not in this life span, then maybe in the next body? If not, that's fine too.

Dear Pop, this is written from you and for you…Super big love and light in your life. Thank you so much for co-creating a beautiful garden space for us children to flourish, un-spoilt like a wild flowers, growing as best as I/we can.

The Ride

My journey began with the secret of change. I was done focusing all my energy on fighting the old. Sarah wanted to build the new. I just couldn't tolerate another four finger whiskey shot at 6am in the morning. I had hollow legs and a numbness in the heart, I simply felt dead. So Pop, as you know, the whiskey all supped, the tears, I had cried me a river, cue song ;-) checkmate, all done.
But what to do? Find a solution but where to start?

I felt that out of compassion, from deeply feeling another's suffering, came the ability to transcend it…Meaning Sarah had to become present, become real. Still relatively asleep at this point, Sarah felt more in a state of arousal as if something was stirring within.
Plus, Monkey Mind kept peeking over my shoulder, chattering away, telling me how undercooked I was, how much work I had to do on myself. So I chose to stay open to it, knowing full well it was going to get painful at times but obviously it was work that I needed/had to do.
So Sarah decided to stay with it, to trust it, to resolve to stay open minded and soft and very present. Oh boy, there was lots of hard work to do.

Living in this 21st Century as an overburdened packhorse, dominated by a male Shiva persona…Whoahhh…time to leave this form of expression. Pack your bags. Female Shakti has to find her way in. She must return to the very essence of her forgotten, pure self. Simply put, I could no longer hold onto this mask any longer, I wanted to embrace the divine feminine, softer nature within. Game on.

During a clear out, a stumbling upon some old baby pictures uncovered a pretty fascinating collection of recorded memories that, when spread out, fan-like on the table revealed the most joyous, chubby, blue eyed cutie with a mop of golden curls. Every single photo, she beamed and radiated pure joy, with an added glimpse of cheeky personality peeking through. You remember the types of photos you used to pose for as a kid? By sticking your tongue out at camera, as if in rebuff, back in the day? The refusing to 'look pretty' for the sake of the ego kind of photograph? Not like today's 'selfie' trout pout, catch your best angle, and take it 10 times to capture the best version of you to upload, expand and share with life to project a great lifestyle?

More pics revealed a soft, gentle, divine little girl, all smiling and girly. Wow-where did she go? I must find her, return to her. Set me free from these shackles as a male, dominating illusion. Sarah is going home.

Right now the ball was set into play. She relinquished her professional work commitments. Her head wasn't in the correct space anyway, not since the emotional passing of her beloved father. Life felt far too fragile and precious.

Next… no next…pause…breathe… be still within and without… for one moment….one moment…. Aha!…Light bulb comes flashing on again…. Figuring my inner passion for autobiographies, stemming from a wondrously funny childhood favourite, The Secret Diary of Adrian Mole 13.5 Years, combined with the beautifully presented film/Book of Eli - how I loved Denzel Washington as an actor, so powerful, so charming in delivering God's hidden message - was Sarah about to culminate the 2 stories through her own experiences? Who even suggested that?

What she did do, however, on a practical level, was buy a blank, A4 lined notebook - the softback kind for lighter travelling - plus plenty of pens and highlighters.

Okay, meditate, return to the clear, blue, quiet sky that you are. Clouds form and pass just like our emotions, both only temporary. In silence, what does the inner guidance system feel, suggest a longing, a desire for? Does the consciousness reveal itself? Adventure, change, growth, excitement, self- enquiry, but where?

That's when the magic of the internet revealed itself in all its splendid glory, enhanced by inner-net, get it…inner net! Hahaha ;-) Good one, Monkey Mind! Back of the net!

Several clicks later, emails have pinged into cyber space and airline tickets are confirmed. Sarah is going on a 4 day Well Women's Retreat programme in Northern Spain, promising daily yoga activities, delicious green juice smoothies, sunrise walks and meditation. Perfect.

Two days later, the bags are packed, though the stomach is feeling kind of jittery in the bag packing, organizing process. "That's the sign of the divine, my lovely," my inner guidance system lovingly whispered.

It had been such a long time since I had done anything like this. Early in my teenage years I would take off on mini solo adventures, but nothing like this. I never had the time to pluck my eyebrows properly without a cute, small toddler demanding my attention, let alone escape, yes escape, alone, on a retreat with other 'solo travellers.' That's the hip terminology for us crazy bitches that do stuff like this, you know, outside the norm, whatever that is. Women just don't go off temporarily and leave their children for their own enjoyment and for purely selfish reasons, for self growth independent of their children's needs, do they?

Do you realize how senseless that even sounds?

Imagine someone saying to you,

"How could you be so selfish that you would choose happiness over me?"

Yet, how can anyone demand that you choose them over your own happiness? To love someone at the cost of your own happiness and they return the love at the cost of their own happiness = 2 unhappy people! That's love, love, love.

Unfortunately, this is the result of our past conditioning, programming and collection of past experiences. In truth, we have been taught to place our happiness in another, giving them the responsibility and ownership of our happiness.

Time to settle yourself, hand passport over, yes physically, even if sweating and shaking profusely. A quick glimpse around indicates no familiar face, no-one to banter with about standing in the longest and slowest queue. No one to demand impatiently and at least 6 times,

"Have you got the air tickets, are you sure?"

A little voice prompted me, "Nerves are the sign of the divine, my lovely." Breathe, slowly and steadily. Inhale, exhale. This is a gift to you and for you, enjoy.

"Yes please, I would like a window seat," a little voice within replied, rather nervously and to the most glamorous airport attendant ever witnessed at that hour of the day.

"Have a lovely time," came the purring, red stained lips.

I smiled within and without…I couldn't wait to sit in my window seat and gawp out the window because I could, at nothing, at everything. In just allowing myself the luxury of simply being. Bliss…

Arghhh, I settled into my seat, becoming familiar with airline logo comfort blanket. No, I wouldn't be taking this to use on beach. The logo is way too obvious and other people with think I was a right cheapskate for stealing it. A sudden thought flashed through my mind - the complimentary earphones and eye mask would come in handy though. Wasn't brought up in the city of Liverpool, or Loverpool, for nothing, laaa.

In my childhood days, we had to glue the milk bottles down in case they got nicked!

Deep sigh of relief, wow, I felt like my namesake, princess. Yes, Sarah does really mean princess. I was freely able to allow myself to choose, to sit, to stand, to fidget, to walk to the bathroom, to disturb my fellow passengers several times, to ask for another, yes another, packet of gummy bears because Sarah wanted to shove more sugar in her big, fat, juicy, emotional face.

Interestingly, as the flight progressed, Sarah started to notice how she moved, how she observed, what she perceived and curiously, started to feel a real taste of freedom about her being. For the first time in a very long time she started to feel the self.

Wellness & Detox Mindfulness: Spain

Tripadvisor, you misleading commodity you. A short distance from the airport is stated, less than half an hour you claim.

Well, destination 'paradise', I had finally arrived (several hours later and after a full coach tour of the whole resort of Benidorm). Including both the contrast of the crumbling old and symmetrical modern parts of the new. Complete with teeth-clenching jaw ache and with sweaty palms from fiddling with my fingers so intently.

Within, I was carrying so much hope that the traveller recommendations lived up to scratch: incredible value for money, blissful, most accommodating, lovely staff, feeling energized and rejuvenated…not much to ask for?…

On first impression, upon sheepishly entering the Retreat Centre doors, I couldn't make my mind up if I had walked into a psychiatric ward dining hall or not. The snapshot I was greeted with was a jamboree of colourful, quirky intensity and of predominately feminine energy.

However, it did possess a smattering of male verve in the heavy oak, rustic dining table and chairs and very typical Spanish decor.

Monkey Mind questioned as to whether it could deliver all the suggested intentions advocated on the glorious web. Mind couldn't quite rationalize.

A brief, 'Hello' from fellow patient, ermmm, I mean paying guest, abruptly welcomed me. One hand wielded a half munched baguette, whilst the other fiddled with wheat crumbs, foaming at the mouth and the elastic, sloppy waistband, barely covering a protruding, swollen, pregnant stomach. Evidently, popping out over the top of her bright, purple, velour 1990's tracksuit bottoms.

Annie proceeded to follow with her professional spiel; list of degrees, accomplishments and basically psychological warfare and resulting meltdown from culminating personal factors.

Woeful, large, brown Asian eyes greeted me with a wistful nod, from the direction of a comfy shaped L lounge space, seemingly unexpressive and very closed. Interesting observation.

The bubbly, vibrant female desk clerk handed me a set of keys to room number 1, very symbolic and mystical if you're into sacred numerology and all that, like me.

Beaming with lioness brood pride, it didn't take more than a few minutes to know her life story. Her dissatisfaction with the Spanish schooling system, her difficulties returning to UK with her Spanish husband, coupled with her career progression.

Can a round peg ever fit into a triangular hole? Not so sure? But, I bet the experience and opportunity to try is certainly a hoot though!

Immediate reaction to the general feel and energy of the place? Mixed. As sisters, lets all open up, share our individual stories. Why had life brought us together at this precise point in time? How can we connect close and deeply so as to help each other, in such a short space of time too? Did I detect a sense of urgency in others or was that just me?

Room number 1, right next to reception and in old courtyard, elaborately styled, complete with ornate, square swimming pool with gorgeous blue and green aquatic tiled designs, mimicking the crisp, clear, Mediterranean waters there. I had fallen on my feet!

A very beautifully fragranced jasmine intertwined a stunning, clematis climbing shrub, idly hung over each doorway, as if hugging all guests together in oneness.

Inside, the room was equally pleasing, typically Spanish in décor, cosy, colourful, homely, with matching blankets and bedding. The soft cushions and colour coordinated furnishings added a warm glow to the stark, white, confrontational, plastered bare walls and minimalistic power shower room.

A long, soapy, powerful, hot shower cleansed my physical form and the soap suds carried any tension away down the spiraling plughole. My shoulders and neck felt immense. Checked reflection in religious looking gilted mirror, not bad for a forty something mum of 2. All 61kg of me, with slightly puffy cheeks and sagging chip shop, bingo wings. Once a feeder, always a feeder I thought. However, on the plus side, my kids always loved Sarah's special homemade chips.

Anyway, I noticed rather dimply, heavy knee fat bulging over my knee caps, reflecting an equally protruding, saggy bottom, with cascading fat rolls running down the back. This was the expected 'norm' for a woman of my age, a conditioned 'norm.' Did I feel at ease with myself? Sarah sure did. I didn't mind what reflected back at me physically, I had earned every squidgy roll.

Carry on judging other people too, you have come a long way thus far, you are allowed to. Your ego has brought you here. Monkey Mind is going to have the best vacation ever. You will be fixed here, or so Sarah thought. Sarah didn't really need that much healing, just rest, good nourishment, just a break from the 'norm.' She will return home to her obligations as a dutiful wife soon enough. She will be fixed, good as new, a better model, no problem.

Evening dinner, check, no wine being served here. I usually took a glass of wine with dinner. First hurdle. Second hurdle…wait for food. Help serve it to the other fellow guests too. Serve others first, enjoy chit chat, connect to smiling chef on presenting such a hearty range of colourful, nutritious, hearty dishes. Don't pick, scoff, stuff into gob as fast as possible because one is emotionally eating oneself to death. For I had something else to crack on with, to be occupied with, that time would not allow any digestion or social interaction to occur.

Plus, the interesting contrast of personality synergy emitted from the husband and wife co-owners held my gaze with intrigue. Was I able to open up that freely? Give my story over that easily? I thought hard, whilst slowly and mindfully rolling the nut roast over the taste buds. Third hurdle. Shit. This feels a bit too much already. Bloody hell. What is Sarah doing here? Slow down. Monkey Mind shut up! Stop laughing and joking and pointing that chubby, hairy finger of yours in my contorting face, suggesting that I made a whopping big mistake.

My hands unconsciously or sub-consciously, started slapping the air, as if an angry wasp was buzzing around the head and ready to launch. What Tom foolery indeed. The detox programme hadn't even started yet. I was only a day in. Gee-whiz. I was already having difficulty surrendering.

As the evening ensued, surprisingly, Sarah became aware of a slight shift away from mind chatter to a little, quieter place within. Sarah became aware of how she sat, her body language, how she ate, chewed her food, swallowed, lifted her glass for more water from the jug, as if all in slow motion. Oh my goodness, what was happening? What was she experiencing? Even to the point of placing the knife and fork down with care and attention and with respect for the food that had just been mindfully eaten. Sarah was experiencing a very new sensation indeed.

Throughout dinner, James, the co-owners husband, magnetized Sarah, not just physically but emotionally too. Sarah had never heard a male being openly speak so directly from the heart space before, with genuine empathy and compassion for others, without rushing off to do something else or other. A fourth. Male species that are open and sensitive and in touch with their feminine side. Beautiful. He talked openly and honestly about his shared experiences in Asia with his gentle wife. He spoke of sharing Silent Vipassana Meditation Retreats, in separate male/female quarters. Both experiencing self and witnessing and observing the pain, the joy and the individual internal healing of self, as and when it arose in unique form, both simultaneously aware and concerned of the others presence. Wonderful.

This planted a seed deeply within, Monkey Mind suggested it sounded like torture and would rather have his eyes scooped out with a spoon. That he would rather the 'me' be sitting at home, on my comfy fat ass, wearing my comfy pj's, marking school work, with a glass of the red stuff in hand and multi tasking whilst watching the latest Coronation Street episode. That, to be blunt, a 10-hour daily meditation programme would kill him and that sitting in the lotus position for that long would kill the 'me' too. Not to mention asking permission for bathroom breaks with my leaky bladder.
Is this couple for real, normal even?

Sarah snuggled under her duvet with rather ruffled feathers that night. A very light, lucid sleep kept her under the realms of a dizzying fairground carousel ride of unfamiliar, red faces and they were spinning round and round with her body slap bang in the middle. Sarah was forced to observe every intense facial expression. Was this dream symbolic or merely my left-side brain's conditioned way of making some sort of sense of my new, unfamiliar surroundings?

Awakening to beautiful rays of warming, Mediterranean light, streaming through the windows, Sarah had a graceful, feline stretch, she had slept well after all.

A pen and small notebook on the bedside locker pulled her to record the night's slightly disturbing images. A feeling, a need to jot down these musings, and thus, a collection of dream diary entries began.

Job done, I slipped out of my warm cocoon and wiggled my hips over to the awaiting metallic, phallic symbol of water joy.

"I feel good, ddddnnnn, like I know that I should, ddddnnnn, so good, so good." I sang loudly as I bathed in the purifying jets of cleansing, hot, delicious water, before setting a morning intention to be very present and observe even more closely this day.

An organic, fruity smell wafted from the dining hall, enticing me over to nourish my inners for a great start to the day.

"Good morning lovely, sleep well?" Sang Sarah, feeling highly energized.

Wee, Scottish pixie girl smiled back shyly as I helped myself to a thick, green, gooey beaker of kryptonite.

"Add some Spirulina to your juice for a healthy boost," wee Scottish girl whispered. Well she didn't say how much so I dolloped a huge tablespoon in and then another half for good measure. Greedy Sarah's belly.

"Mm mm, very earthy tasting on the palette, grainy too, thanks," I chuckled as I mindfully sipped my gloop.

"You're welcome," wee Scottish girl replied with a huge grin in her eyes. Maybe she wasn't so painfully shy after all, just timid, Sarah thought briefly, maybe slightly mischievous too?

Within an hour of ingestion, 24 hours of vomiting and diarrhea plagued Sarah's body. Understood the wee grin, on wee Scottish girl's face now all too well. Sarah had over- dosed on Spirulina, which gave the physical body much quicker purification than anticipated. Free from toxins internally but how about the mind? How does one clean that?

A few hours later, Sarah dragged herself away, temporarily, from her porcelain bowl of impurities and crawled into the kitchen into the open, friendly arms of our Dutch Chef Ami, for a much needed cuddle and to offload even more words that troubled the mind.

Sarah's conditioned mind would ease sickness by eating 'binding' bland foodstuffs like scrambled egg, rich tea biscuits and hot buttered toast, not prana. Prana?

Chef Ami went on talking about life or prana and how it can be obtained from many sources for nourishment.

You're telling me that the body doesn't always need food for sustenance? That it can survive off sea minerals? That the food you eat becomes the body? That the gut has highly receptive neurons which transmit to the brain to tell you how you're feeling? How the food you eat has feelings that in turn affect you?

Sarah thought she was in a nut house, hallucinating from the bout of sickness, dehydrated even. A vegetarian nuthouse. What is this bullshit? I could just imagine sharing this advice with my kids when they got sick. I could imagine the look of complete astonishment on their faces.

No, these nice people meant well. Sarah didn't understand. She came from a very different reality. In her world folk shopped on a Sunday, washed on a Monday, made love on a Tuesday, ate takeaway food on a Friday and Saturday, washed down with copious amounts of wine and titillating reality game shows. Happy evenings.

Namaste…The body loved the various yoga classes on offer. It responded deeply to the stimulation and movement of energy though the joints creaked. Luckily, Sarah thanked her body for the effort and didn't beat herself up about it.

Did I nail Dancer pose today? Or did I fall over, notice it, observe how it felt and then let it go? There is no winning or losing in yoga. This Sarah quickly learnt.

It was here, in Spain, that the delights of kundalini yoga were first sampled, with all its glorious oohing and erring and channeling and high energetical sexual functions. Not to mention the sassy moves demonstrated from a curvaceous, olive skinned yogini, wearing a gorgeous, hot, deep pink, satin, thong leotard. Made Sarah blush it did.

What an experience though! Did I feel an electrical current running up and down my spine? No, but I certainly did follow the class with a prompt search on the all- knowing web about Yoga.

The result? Many beautiful quotes from Swami Sivananda:

"By our stumbling the world is perfected."

"The attitude of gratitude is the highest yoga."

Sarah needed to embed these principles into her psyche. She began to realize the significance of the mind/body connection, that what affects the body, affects the mind and vice versa. Feeling in the practice itself, how one breathes mindfully and then relaxes. Allowing one to let go of limiting beliefs and self imposed barriers.

Yoga had it all. Sarah become hooked and a yoga junkie over night.

Yin, Vinyasa, Hatha, Ashtanga and Yoga Nidra. Sarah tried them all with incredible joy and with wonderfully patient, knowledgeable teachers. The very nature of these enriching lessons, developed a fresh renewed sense of independent freedom, by being able to explore how the body surrendered to each discipline very differently. What no one talked about though was how the busy mind had nowhere to go during 3-minutes of settling in to Butterfly pose. At first, mind really, really complained but after a while it gave up. It got sick of doing the shopping, asking what it wanted to eat next, of asking why was I here, etc., etc.? It started to settle down, soften and go with the flow.

Much like having free range access in a sweet shop. To indulge or not to indulge? Touché.

Welcome to the world of 'Happy Baby,' this asana making Sarah's body feel very vulnerable and exposed.

Didn't know what Annie was thinking when she got into this posture either, or how for that matter, with her heavily swollen abdomen. Was her baby about to pop out too? Would we soon be presented with a real life happy baby?

After a soothing practice and a guided meditation with the lovely, gentle Nicole, wife of super hottie James, boom! The mask slipped off temporarily and underneath, revealed a glimpse of the girly self I thought I'd lost. Uncontrollable tears rolled down the cheeks, but Sarah felt over-whelmingly happy and at peace at the same time. How did that happen?

For starters, let me recreate the scene...
The collective consciousness is still. The yogis are sitting in easy pose or lotus. Lavender essential oil and sweet body odour permeates the air and warming sun rays cascade through the large, south facing patio window to soothe the body further. Nicole comfortingly whispers a guided meditation based on mental imagery. The theme is based on flying high in the air on a magic carpet and feeling the presence of someone close by. That was an easy task. That was you, Dad.
A conscious memory from childhood surfaced.
Most interestingly, I hadn't been on a flying carpet since I was 10years old. Each bedtime, and for a short while during my dream state, as a kid Sarah would sail out of her bedroom window, above the rooftops, high into the clouds for a nightly adventure, remembering the silence and stillness of the night sky and loving it.
This memory triggered a deep sense of love within my heart and the tears flowed out of the corners of my eyes, softly rolling down my cheeks as if to caress them. The grief hit me and yet very lovingly escaped from my eyes.
Sarah had heard other people talk of loss of loved ones before. Felt their pain, identified with their grief but never did realize just how significant a loved one's death can affect the physical body. Not until you left your physical body, Dad.

Never fully understood how the body stores memories through the senses, through the smell, personal touch, sound/tones of voice and their feel. This is all that's left when a body leaves you. Gone. No shared intimacy, no talk of forgiveness, no apology, no final goodbyes, that is reserved for the blessed ones. Just to be left with a heavy heart loaded with sensory memories.
"Who is joining me for 5am sunrise walk in the morning?" Came an eager distant voice from across the kitchen worktops, whilst lovingly and furiously chopping away the evenings mixed, root vegetables.

"Go on then," Sarah sluggishly replied, even though deep down still feeling Happy baby and savouring its embrace.

"Great, meet you in the lobby at 4:45am sharp," beamed Chef, "And don't forget, I'll provide provisions, you provide yourself."

Bedtime was going to come early for Sarah.

As she left the dinner table, after helping clear the plates, James came by and plopped something into her lap.

"Enjoy this," he directed, adding, "If this doesn't resonate with you, that's fine but give it a go." End of conversation.

Our previous evenings 1:1 silent meditation, dark, silent and still, sat cross legged opposite each other on meditation cushions and eye gazing, implied to Sarah that he was more than hot and not just eye candy. He had the most beautiful, soft dark curls, gentle hazel eyes and an inviting, infectious grin. Plus, his heart was so sensitive too, he really listened. Sarah wanted to ask him outright if his partnership was open? Would he kiss her back if she leaned in? Why was her heart racing?

The purpose of the silent meditation was self enquiry. Naughty Monkey Mind you almost got me into trouble again. Shut up! Re-focus, look within.

Well anyway, she liked his worldly, masculine presence. She would take a peek at a few pages of his book, to satisfy her enquiring mind. Anthony De Mello-Awareness 1986.

Later that evening, Sarah snuggled into bed, garment free, opened the book and started to read page 1,2,3…. p76 within a few hours. Fact: Life had dropped into the lap and shared the most important book that would alter my very perception of being and, simply put, change my life. Each and every beautiful word on the page, construed together, simplistically phrased, similes and metaphors, language and delivery, jumped out to hug Sarah with a full on universal, perfectly timed, colossal squeeze. Fuelling the fire to support Monkey Mind's theory of my 'undercookedness.'

The reality that Sarah had been living in no longer served her. The trauma of her father's passing had sent her soul flying into the cosmos in search of truth.

THAT book was to become the Pandora's box. Once opened, any inquisitive mind could not close. A giant 'wet willy' had slapped her in the face, the path of consciousness, of awareness began to ripen…

By day 3. More troubled sleep and tossing and turning, the body is squirming. Monkey Mind is having a field day. You can't go for a walk at this hour, it's ridiculous, your eyes can't focus in the dark. He is throwing a lot of stuff at me.

4:30am, the theme tune to Dirty Dancing goes off. Time to get up. Although I'm not dancing. Mind is suggesting Sarah will go hungry without filling up on carbs, especially walking up a mountain side. What if…what if…what if…

A grumpy Sarah goes to meet a chirpy Chef in the lobby. Chef is always smiling and full on raring to go. What is this woman on? Anti-depressants? Crack?

"Are any other guests joining us?" I quizzed.

"Not sure," came the chirpy, abrupt reply. We wait 5 more minutes before proactive Chef makes a democratic decision and decides to leave. "Their loss."

She throws on her puffer jacket with zest and off we set, out into the cool morning streets, winding in and out of small backstreets aiming for the wooded mountain entrance.

Sarah's eyesight appears to be getting worse. The early morning darkness, the unexpected cars pulling out from desolate side streets and residential cats jumping out from under stationary cars made the physical body irritable and jumpy. Chef was not perplexed in the slightest. Why did I feel this way and she didn't?

Our pace quickened as we eventually found a forest opening after crossing an unlit, empty car-park. We jumped over a tiny stream and made our way through a tiny gap in an unsecure, manmade makeshift fence. Our ascent began.

Having never experienced woodland in the dark before, I sensed a sharp pang of previous darkness traumatization. Trees cast an eerie shadow overhead and all around. No significant outline could be made of any noun in the distance, just the imminent tarmac observed under foot.

"Ami, Ami," I shrieked, "Look ahead in the distance, there is a big, black wolf charging towards us!" I screamed as I grabbed her arm to pull me in closer.

She roared. "Sarah, my dear, it is a male jogger in black sweatpants."

Okay so he's a rapist, Monkey Mind quickly informed me. Two meters, one, 0.5, he breezed past us. Phew...I'd known my eyes were getting bad but not this bad. This was a new level. What a fool. What was mind thinking?

Ami started to tell Sarah about the local history of the area, how it held significant training opportunities for runners and cyclists alike to increase endurance in nature. Lesson learnt. Let go, breathe, enjoy.

Ami calmly spoke, "Wait until we reach the top of the mountain and watch the sunrise. If we're lucky enough we may catch a glimpse of dolphins too."

Ami handed a breathless Sarah a rewarding, nourishing, green juice as we sat together on the rock face in silence, to witness the most glorious unfolding that I had ever seen from such height. A timeless and effortless motion, gliding upwards, casting a huge, golden shining presence, forming a sensational, vibrational light source across the twinkly ocean like a powerful light sabre. At this point, Sarah did not care for a dolphin spectacular, she was far more mesmerized by that golden globe of superpower in the sky. In a split second, one felt such an immediate force of recognition and momentous understanding about that there thing suspended in the sky, which infinitely beams all life creation.

Ami, through your silence you share so much wisdom. How can that be?

"Fancy doing a vision board, followed by a guided meditation I'm running later, my darling?" Ami winked back as if she appreciated my thoughts.

"Sounds fun, why not," I replied.

Did our friend Annie want to join too? Not really. Like the others guests, she had her own schedule.

In addition, when I suggested it to her, she informed me that she had a date arranged with a full fat litre bottle of coke, Brie and more French bread. It was obviously proving difficult to stick to the vegetarian, carb less diet plan for her. It's a shame, though. When pregnant you do suffer the most incredible cravings. I remember my preference- munching soil from the garden.

Annie shuffled off into the direction of the supermarket, mumbling on about some educational crisis or other and she certainly didn't want to know about the sunrise walk or the hidden Lighthouse and the secret hidden reading spot. A real gem of a find, total seclusion down a little track to the water's edge. Plus, only a 20 minutes walk away on foot. No traffic to navigate, no long stretches of motorway, just simple God-given legs, reached simply by placing 1 foot in front of the other and voilà, a new contrasting experience. Relaxed and content, I dozed off in my womblike, comfortable bed. Felt such peace and tranquility after the morning sunrise walk. Upon reflection, things seemed to be taking on a new meaning, a new definition, a new way of looking at things. Felt another kind of little, magical shift going on somewhere deep inside of my being some more. I liked it too and wanted/ needed more. Sarah in Indian means greedy, wanting more. Yes, that's Sarah for you, that's me. The evening meal was the most delicious and fresh homemade, veggie, pot roast that I had ever tasted. A real tasty mouthful after mouthful for sure. The food tasted alive and full of vitality. Before, I hadn't realized that in blessing the food, expressing gratitude for one's nourishment, that it actually enhances the cellular structure of the substance. Food becomes the body. We absorb it all. We are not what we eat but what we absorb and all that! Sarah was learning!

It did help too, that Ami had lovingly prepared, chopped, blended and whistled so much love and joy into every meal. Fascinating woman, so inspirational. Her story told of faraway friendships in Nepal, of a Guru, of living in a tipi on the mountain rocks in Hawaii and sailing with a Turkish crew and as personal sous chef around the Mediterranean Sea. Her reflections of her journey made great bedtime stories and gave me the greatest longing and burning desire to experience the same. After many, many years of devotional child rearing and balancing a tight ship, these stories were musical symphonies.

Unconscious at this point of any real deeper shift in my soul body, I simply thought I was going on a short break to a lovely location. For sure, this new experience ticked all the right boxes to relax, to reconnect the physical body and experience some self love. Then after this 'me time' I would be able to return to my mother bound duties, 3D reality, nothing is possible and same same. Husband reiterated the same... Sarah believed it wholeheartedly too.

Later in the evening, after a beautiful meditation stroll along the beach, admiring lovers connecting intimately under the warmth of the suns rays, Ami promptly reminded us about the evenings workshop, much like a governess would do rounding up her pride.
We gathered into the Yoga Hall, like lambs to slaughter, to be met by a very intriguing array of objects. Instantly, I realized a lot of effort had been put into this programme, a lot of attention and care, of which the outcomes were unknown.

Previously, in school I had planned numerous lessons for kids, obviously some more engaging and exciting than others. But something within my teacher persona suggested this was a different kind of teaching altogether, more sacred to the self. It pricked my ears up with intrigue and excitement and it seemed plenty of fun too! On the teacher side, for me, the guidelines were a little too heavy. Rules given; to sit in opposite corners of the hall, with no eye contact or speaking allowed. Ami would give instruction as to when we could select resonating pictures from carefully chosen magazines that sat neatly in a pile in the center. An A5 sugar paper sheet given, which would be the frame template so as to hang the visual projections of subconscious desires on.
But first, a beautifully spoken guided meditation with equally beautiful music played, to allow us all to come together in that quiet stillness. Still quite new to this meditation malarkey, I kept doing it although not really knowing its full implications. It just made Sarah feel calm and relaxed. Sixty minutes later, the workshop had come to a close, the requested instructions abided by. Sarah had mindfully, diligently, selected the desired magazine phrases and pictures, had carefully cut out and stuck them down in an artistic, spider map fashion. Upon observation, what an interesting spectacle of pictorial thoughts. Ami directed another shorter guided meditation so as to 'settle the energy.' Sarah was getting used to this term a lot more now. Energy this, energy that, energy, energy, energy. Think life was trying to tell me about the importance of energy, due to a huge lack of awareness about it.

As a teacher, I did teach many science lessons across the key stages. But for me, energy was simply, in context, electricity, gas, wind turbines or fossil fuel. My version of energy stayed in that box of reality. At the time, that box of reality was real my friends, until much later, when the divine spoke and shattered all my preconceived illusions.

The box is created by mind, a clever conditioned, secret programme within the psyche so as to inhibit expansion and growth for truth. A hidden golden nugget of a reality, available to all if so desired. And not purchased from a fast food joint either!

Little did Sarah know what would follow a few months later. As suggested, upon returning home, this vision board was placed in a significant spot on an old, imported Indian chess table. Astonishingly quickly, noting how these pictures on this vision board actually started to manifest. How could this be possible? Is this a form of black magic or witchcraft something? Dear God, what was happening? What have I gotten myself into now? I was challenging my Monkey Mind constantly, sending emails back and forth to clarify and check my questioning. Was I losing my grip?

Remember the days in school, when you naughtily did an Ouija board at playtime and sneakily in the toilets?

One of the group, and usually female, would cry out hysterically because you had contacted her absent father? Remember feeling that deep-rooted fear at being found out? From…. A. Breaking the girls heart. B. Playing with the devil. C. Parents finding out. D. Getting expelled from school. Oh the shame of it! Back in the day when authority actually scared kids and parents had a leg to stand on and could smack them for discipline.

Sarah distinctly remembers getting the slipper across her buttocks and a few cracks around the head, yet remains undisturbed by these experiences as an adult?

Life seemed to be slipping from my fingers. I was losing control and no longer in the driving seat. Somehow, I had relinquished control and surrendered to something within. Sarah can't find the right words to explain. Just that she knew something, no words, many words, she just felt different.

"What is this religious bullshit, you are listening to?" Hubby demanded. Upon returning home, I found these newly found mantras warming and uplifting, giving me a spring in my step, to clean and polish the big, old, Victorian home.

"This is a load of American brainwashing shite!" He added on hearing my new found friends, Esther Hicks and cohort Abraham.

Sarah, on the other hand, rather enjoyed snuggling down in the darkness of her candle lit study, wrapped in cosy blankets, sipping lemon honey tea. Spiritually bypassing any emotions coming up, too. He, meanwhile, still enjoyed drinking in the pub and came home humming of cigarettes and alcohol. Cue Oasis lyrics. These are acts of non self love. Bless.

Not my story, not my place to say. We each have our own karmic path to walk and with different ways of travelling there. Anyway, Sarah had experienced enough of this self loathing, no more alcohol or toxins in this body for her. Her chakra wheels were spinning nicely.

The internal shift had begun. This was a very cathartic moment, for a new softer, feminine Sarah was about to bloom. Like the Cluedo board game, Sarah evolved into the character of Miss Black. Sarah Black her pseudonym name. Ask my mother Doris, what colour I painted all my bedroom walls as a teenager? Go on, she loves telling that tale. Why of course...black, black walls, doors, wardrobes the lot. I went through a real dark phase, so much so that even my hair got dyed to match!

Sarah launched into the Cluedo mystery, Full Metal Jacket style, on a mission to solve a mission. My YouTube inner net search revealed a whole host of enlightened beings, each with different expression of the same source: Mooji, Adyashanti, Bentinho, Esther Hicks, Aisha Salem, Osho, Geoff Thompson and the lovely Dr. David Hawkins. To name but a few inspiring, enlightened souls. Thank you for sharing.

You ever get the feeling when you want something new, say a red VW golf, and then all you ever see are red VW Golf's? That's life speaking in volumes lovely being. Sarah had thought that she had found hen's teeth. How come I had never heard of this way of sharing from the heart before? I, he, she, Sarah, Monkey Mind whatever, we loved this form of expression and became hooked, good and proper like an old Chubb fish, a great fisherman's catch.

Down Dog, Up Dog, stack vertebrae on vertebrae…"Don't run at the wall to do handstand, you look like an over eager child." So many words after words…oh my goodness! Sarah was getting tired. Her favourite yoga classes had become lifeless, heartless and emotionless. A thin, transparent veil had slipped away, greedy Sarah wanted more. Monkey Mind confirmed this. You can do better, yoga is not just for the 20-year-old something's, sporting tight lycra on beautiful tight bodies, HD brows and immaculate silky hair.

Sarah's inner guru rolled her eyes at the lack of yoga instructors over 40 years, wearing thicker set bodies with leaky pelvic floor muscles from childbirth and sporting grey, sage strands running through the hair line. Not the Marc Jacobs handbag jet set, more like a M&S bag for life tribe.

Monkey Mind was conjuring up a plan, Sarah could feel it in the pit of her stomach. A few clicks later after a brief whistle stop trip around the Interglobe, over a nice, steaming cup of hot coffee, Sarah had done it. She had confirmed herself a place on a 200 hour Hatha Yoga course Ancient Patanjali Style in Rishikesh; a holy city in Northern India, world famous for inspiring all spiritual yogi beings. Even The Beatles had an Ashram built there. Scousers, can get where water can't, they can…lol.

Online, the Ashram looked beautiful, nestled away in some tiny, quirky back street, a stroll away from the Mother of all rivers, the Holy Ganges. The Teacher seemed genuine, supported holistic medicine and dedicated his service to deprived, sick children in hospitals and orphanages. This guy suggested a heart of gold. Price was affordable too. Winner, winner chicken dinner!

Dad, I'm off. All 63kg of me. Okay my weight had gone up a little. Rucksack packed, visa obtained.

Hubby again repeated his mantra, "Ok, go in search of yourself but come back and settle into reality this time."

Famous last words.

A tender, loving hug at the airport followed a request for an Instagram picture. Reluctantly, I half- smiled, but was very glad of a lift to the airport and small talk to hide anyy anticipation of my impending challenge. Another solo trip but a tad further and longer this time, all 6 glorious weeks away and half way around the world too. Not bad for a girl, who, up until a few months ago, couldn't walk to the shops on her own in the dark, let alone catch a plane! Why did I feel this strong urge/desire to go? Love. Simply that. Sarah had started to fall in love with herself.

Openly, I hate society's trend of picturing and capturing everything and anything to blog; every second of every day from clothes to each food item consumed. Who cares? Back off! I'd rather live in the present and enjoy than share it amongst so- called friends so as to glorify the lavish, ego self. Yawn.

In those days, couldn't even take a nap without some cheeky beggar 'Snap Chatting' my ridiculous slobber-drooled face to another. What for? Amusement? Let me be, relaxing in my true self, food stains on my top and all. Life is pretty hectic in 3D.

These days, don't recognize that girl looking back from that Instagram pic. Not the eyes, the body shape, the hair style nor nothing, no-thing at all.

Fortunately, or unfortunately, depending which side of the family you came from, this was the last to be seen of that lovely, toxic girl. Guru Baba of Patanjali Yoga was about to completely change all that.

Om Namah Shivaya.

Indian Delights: The Transformational Yogini

Dazed and confused, after a particularly long long-haul flight, I woke up abruptly from a mini departure lounge nap to a plethora of flashing cell phones and male pearly whites. Now, this was an interesting dream.
Sarah brushed the chapatti crumbs off her chest and glanced up at the overhead monitor to check the times for the connecting flights to Jolly Giant airport. Or some other funny sounding Indian name or other, which was just too mission impossible to pronounce. Noting lots of honeyed number 11's flashing up, a great sign from the angels that I was on track. Wonderful.

A dishwater blond, fully clothed, white female western backpacker was certainly a bemusing sight for these horn dog Indian males. A factor to be witnessed on several occasions throughout this Indian Highlights Tour. Monkey Mind added his 2pence worth in too... Surely these guys had seen a fully clothed middle aged western women before? This is the 21st Century!

Another quick glance up, Sarah observed her rapidly flashing neon numerals. Thirty minutes to pass before the next leg of the tour. Sarah, armed with a spicy chicken wrap and bottle of water, (Girl Guide Motto; always be prepared) dashed across the lounge to another terminal building. One practically levitated across the Aztec carpet lounge runway to momentarily stop for a quick rest in what one could describe as the most anti-quainted s-shaped leatherette chairs, that would look more at home in the Tate Modern than an Indian airport lounge. Sarah felt like a queen embarking on a royal visit, smug not, joyful indeed. This moment felt wonderful, the internal GPS kicked in, hugging the body from within. I smiled, Sarah smiled. She checked her mobile one last time for any last minute text messages from home. None. No-one was concerned about me. Life had created a space for me to be. All good.

However, as the legs boarded the flight, feelings of panic came up, could this be the result of this new found responsiveness? Aka One Direction celebrity status? Photographs, camera phones, click, click, click?

To calm the unsteadiness, and bang on cue universal timing and once again, thank you, my next flight companion eased this tension. For aligned in the window seat next to me sat an incredible Indian gentle giant, who softly spoke about the safest and least expensive way of getting out and about in his beautiful country. Sarah felt a surge of confidence and felt ready for the landing. Lone woman fear syndrome...reject that idea.

"Let battle commence!" So to speak, in the best Alan Partridge voice ever!

Touch down, Sarah had made it. Passport was checked and stamped, ego wanted to build a collection of foreign stamps? Rucksack collected, minus a few more straps, but hey ho, it was the first one off the conveyor belt as asked for this time. Winner, winner chicken dinner. Did Sarah have turrets in a previous life?

HUGE gulp, and I mean huge gulp! As the physical body made its way out of the terminal building and into a waiting cab...and it wasn't from the observed increase of humidity and heat I can tell you...

The heart felt as though it had dropped through the earth with a thud, for who should be stood leaning outside the exit doors, bold as brass, smiling this beautiful, most welcoming smile? Like a true ray of sunshine?

"Welcome to India," beamed my good, old friend Monkey Mind, as he threw me a cold coconut water. Sarah was gob smacked, literally stuck for words and that was a first!

Nervously, jumping into the back of the cab, feeling this male powerful presence and without an exchange of words, heard his suggestions quite clearly.

"This is your test, well done so far but how far are you willing to go for truth?"

Sarah sat rather quietly in contemplation yet her mouth warbled incoherently to the taxi driver? Who senses a full-on duality episode here?

"Shit a brick, this Monkey Mind presence has gained super powers over here!" Heaved Sarah under her breath.

Must be this natural habitat that's doing it; the tropical climate, the fruit trees and the banter from the other wild cheeky rascals freely roaming around exploring, snorting on this powerfully loaded jungle energy she thought.

She also thought this.... What on earth was she doing in the jungle, in a dilapidated taxi with no suspension, rattling up and down over pot holes, dodging women with heavy baskets on their heads, with half clothed little children pooping openly in the streets? She should be at home in the family house preparing the Sunday Lunch, sorting all the washing out and organizing packed lunches for the week ahead. I AM a mother and mothers don't pack up and leave their brood to fend for themselves? Do they?

Amazed at the passing scenery, Sarah stared some more out of the window. She wanted to sit up close to this beautiful Monkey Mind of mine, stroke his delicious prolific jawline and wrap his arm around hers.

Somewhere from the depths of within, a tiny creature roared, "You're just doing real fine, this is right for your soul." Sarah felt like a balanced Libran scale.

A few hours later, and feeling totally engulfed now by this magnificent part of the world, so rich and vibrant in colour, like a continuous tropical painting. Sarah arrived at the sacred city of Rishikesh.

The taxi ride had weaved its way through the hustle and bustle of mopeds, sacred cows, street vendors, spiritual seekers, travellers, beeping cars, beeping buses, spraying dust, Indian ice-lolly sucking family groups, day trippers, sari's, head scarves and well worn flip flops galore. Magical.

Snappishly, the smiley nodding taxi driver came to a sudden halt at an unmarked crossroads, 3 points on a UK license for that prohibited car maneuver, mind prompted, as he motioned his head towards a thin passageway in the distance. Sarah got out to pay, rather nervously looking ahead at the lack of overhead street lights and gaping big holes underfoot, passing underground waste. Interesting projection of a late night accident occurring, nice one, reject that idea right away.

The back pack was thrown over the shoulder and off Sarah wandered, contact name and yoga ashram info in one hand, a big, nervous smile in the other.

Suddenly, after a leisurely 5-minute stroll in deliciously lethargic heat, a bold phallic building, symbolic of strength and power, popped up, right there in front of the eyes. Wow, such an expression of male Shivaness that looked so much bigger and bolder in real life. Sarah felt like a tiny ant. She had arrived.

The ornate metallic balconies and grandiose design seemed to escalate forever, though there felt a real softness and devotional aspect to the place, added to by the pastel hand painted Hindu images circling the entrance, safeguarding a huge, impressive, heavy cast iron door. Instantly, she felt the love poured into those.
Sarah was welcomed into a dimly lit marble hallway with a gently cascading waterfall feature holding corner space of a stark, otherwise bare wall.

A broad smile, with an added air of mischief, greeted and seated her being in a small, cosy room, adorned with vibrant traditional Asian pink and orange brightly coloured sequined cushions.
"Welcome to Rishikesh, Sarah!" Enthused guru, dressed head to toe in starch, white clothes, unbelievably clean and manicured too, with a real twinkle in his eyes. A second greeting of the day. Sarah instantly felt sluggish in his presence.
Guru and I exchanged small talk, no lengthy discussion of yoga course expectations however? No discussions of truth, of original source taken from Ancient Yoga Style Sanskrit books?
He was more interested in my UK location and ultimately delighted in expressing his knowledge about Manchester United Football club, as most people do on holiday. Lol.

Funny, Sarah felt immediately at ease in his presence from this very first somewhat succinct (or brief) encounter. His eyes were very soft and gentle and he had such a witty sense of humour for an Indian guy, such a wise crack with poor jokes!

On the web, guru shares his support of local orphanages, schools and hospitals and has a PHD in nutrition for holistic natural healing. Impressive, this guy though, in the flesh, had a heart of gold, one could feel it, and did not sell short his truth. Felt very humbled.

Gut instinct was right too, along with the Monkey Mind who of course helped orchestrate the whole thingamajig as well! Bless!

However, curiously, when it came to the exchange of student fees, Sarah felt her hand quiver. Was this an attachment issue? Last minute nerves and fear of failure kicking in?

A quick glance up noticed the arrival of fellow students, appearing as if by magic, from a puff of smoke from behind the heavy, cast iron doors, bringing more nervous anticipation to the mix. Feeling apprehensive? Straight back at ya....Reflected these random windows of the soul. Sarah would be ok.

After a brief introduction in the yoga and meditation hall, all beings were de-briefed with regard to the strict house rules. The ears digested the information. Monkey Mind hinted on undergoing a 28-day sentence of purification, prison service.

Sarah glanced around the bright and airy practice room, knowing full well that she would spend a lot of time in there. A deep seated, knowledgeable feeling came over her, of previous students' blood, sweat and tears. If this is what it takes to re-connect with the self, the consciousness, God self, then Thy kingdom come, it shall be done.

Eleven mixed European, Middle Eastern and Asian eyes flickered around the room, each with their own story to express, each with their own personal challenges to overcome. Sarah was the only UK national representative. Om Namah Shivaya.

In this Holy city the policy included; no meat, no alcohol, no drink, no drugs, no make-up, no revealing Western Clothes, no chemicals, no late nights but instead good clean Satva, organic wholesome foods and laughter. Does this sound like your idea of fun? Like an all-inclusive 5-star holiday to Tenerife maybe?

It did to Sarah. She felt at home straight away, she loved the purity of it. In fact, she loved waking up to the rising of the sun over the Himalayan mountains in the distance, the way the light expanded and contracted in glowing oranges and yellows across the sky. A stunning wake up call. A true blessing.

Loved hanging out on the balcony for intimate chats, discussing all things bright and beautiful over herb tea. Loved meandering through the mirage of tiny, open cracked alleyways, smiling with joyful school children carrying tiny lunch packs, of donkeys and hay bales and workers carrying huge weights on their heads.

Loved greeting other beings in those little streets and finding little conscious satsangs, with other beings in search of spiritual development. Loved the angelic, melodic mantras floating out from the sacred temples. Loved the cheeky monkeys guarding the connecting bridges, ready to pounce for a passing treat. Loved the tranquility of watching groups of Indian families enjoying their bathing in the Holy Ganges.

Loved the simplicity of the market sellers, squeezing fresh juice from the sides of the dusty roads. Loved the jungle treks and stories of wild tigers and missing children. Of villagers who told of piercing screams in the night when their youngsters were sent for firewood, only never to be seen again. Instead, piles of stones and loving sentiments took their place.

Loved having the time to bless my food and be thankful for every delicious mouthful.

Loved, loved, loved this amazing space. Sarah had never been to such a destination before and was soaking it all up.

Seemed many moons ago, when she was sat at home in front of the Juliet balcony, gazing out at the overcast greyness of North West Lancashire hills, dream trawling the world wide web for a yoga teacher training course. Travelling electronically around the world discovering retreats including; Mexico, Spain, Italy, Turkey, USA and Thailand. You name it, Sarah Googled it. Although Monkey Mind was a darling in this instance, by excitedly pointing a suggestive finger to this sacred place on Google Maps.

Such a sense of joy was felt hanging out with this multicultural bunch. Such a wonderful, eclectic gathering of beautiful beings! The language barriers and verbal communication added so much more fun. Although Sarah did know a bit of French and Spanish, she did not class herself as bilingual, not in the slightest.

Luckily, Guru spoke broken English, although at times, it was tricky to decipher his meaning, let alone in Sanskrit!

Thus the atmosphere created. Could she make the distance? This was not a sprint race but a long distance marathon, she prompted herself on luminous yellow post- it notes above the bed.

Day 2, Day 3 and Day 4...Sick as a dog hallucinating on acid. Another bout of sickness crouched over the porcelain bowl. The body didn't know whether to shit or throw up, or both. Thank God, it was an open plan power shower for easy spillages.

Seriously, this was not envisioned. Could hear the delights of the other yogi students floating up and down the staircase to practice. This was not what Sarah desired. The intensity felt in the stomach was off the Richter scale, and was far more intense than the Spanish sickness episode. This felt like full blown bodily dying.

Day 4, early evening, there comes a loud knock on the door.

"Sarah, how are you?' Guru inquired.

A pathetic appearance and puffy red eyes said it all. Guru passed a packet of charcoal looking pellets.

"Sarah, this is good news, this is purification," smiled Guru as he casually slipped off down the hall. Sarah thought hard. What did he actually mean by that?

Did he empathize with my depths of pain felt? That the body was tormented with so many physical aches and pains, and after only 1 day's practice as well?

Where did that come from? Jet lag? At home Sarah ate reasonably well, cycled weekly. Plus, as a Mum of two could still run for the bus without a swinging arm. She was reasonably fit? Plus, she had not long returned from a detox programme. Surely this was enough preparation?

Evening of Day 4. Sarah suffered many disturbing dreams, half conscious and tossing and turning in the bed. Similar to those in Spain but much more sinister. Deep in the subconscious part of sleep, many faces appeared, clowns, known, un friendly and stoic; playing round and round like a record player, re-appearing then disappearing, fading in and out constantly. Dream diary take note!

As the morning sun passed gloriously by the window, the body half heartedly stumbled out of bed, weak as a kitten and exhausted from lack of food and disturbed sleep. Sarah was not looking forward to a 2.5- hour pranayama and yoga practice, not in the least.

After a few sips of water and a rinsed face, Sarah slipped on her white attire and headed downstairs to a warm welcome and concerned, loving remarks.

Within 20 minutes of practice something deep within clicked into place. Sarah no longer felt sick and needy and lifeless but rather the contrary, switched on, on fire and raring to go.

The flies went un-noticed, the body moved with ease and grace, the time passed so quickly that it felt like a 5-minute session. Funnily, during the guided meditation session, nearing the end, our Guru seemed to be engulfed in a puff of red smoke. Sarah put her glasses back on to check a visibility issue? No it was still there. Our teacher was sat in the lotus position surrounded in a red haze. Freaky!

During the days that would follow, the 62 kg body frame started feeling increasingly awkward, like it wanted to break and shatter into tiny shards of glass. The legs wanted to break completely and physically and they hurt deeply in several postures. The chest area felt like it wanted to be ripped open?

Our guru assured Sarah that this was the body experiencing 'opening...' and not 'pain'...and that the cells liked it and were ecstatically dancing as a result.

At the time, didn't realize that this mantra resonated so deeply within. So much so, that it was to be verbally repeated with Sarah's own yogi students, a few months later.

Dad, wherever your presence is right now in the world. Sarah hopes that you can feel this torture your daughter is putting herself under, both through you and in you. In her heart she knows that she has chosen the right path and that would make us both happy. Somehow, all sense of logic and reasoning has been abandoned, well that typically of the previous Sarah's conditioned being anyway. Is this you too, my/our lovely dear Daddy?

Ooooch!!! Felt that tiny bone click right out of its socket, from a tiny samurai sword wielding Japanese warrior yogini. Gasps echoed around the room for Yoko, our master's pleasant demonstration model for the ever increasingly difficult asanas. Did she flinch or make a sound? Of course not. True warriors don't.

Did he ever choose Sarah? Yes. She was grateful to be flipped upside down, thrown up against the wall, gripped by her ankles, gagging for breath and in total embarrassment of letting out a lady garden fart in front of watchful eyes.

Ever heard the story about Indian guy, who one month into his fast began craving sugarcane? So much so, that mind ordered him out from his abode to go get this drink from the local markets. However, the plot thickens. This guy outsmarted mind. He purchased the said drink and stuck his tongue in it for mind to experience. He did not consume the liquid down his throat, into his belly as mind was demanding.

Same, same as the Babas, whose calling it is to stand up for a lifetime, to walk this earth with an arm raised, to roll in fire, to cover their naked body in ashes, to demonstrate that we are so much greater than the body.

Sarah was just beginning to feel this through her own direct experiences.

Something else started cropping up too. Sarah became aware of the physical bodies other bodies. The etheric and the emotional for starters. That these postures or asanas that we were learning about, weren't just simply a series of flexibility movements to exhibit litheness, oh no, far more to it than that.

For certain, in the West, yoga is portrayed as an exercise, and shamefully so I must say, but in reality is it so much more. In one expression, it is, in laymen's terms, a series of postures and breath techniques which aid chakra healing and energy flow. In another, it is an opportunity, in the wise words of the Dalai Lama, *'The practice of tolerance, of holding on and letting go.'* More so, when one really learns breathing techniques or Pranayama, it positively does affect actions and thoughts. Every thought changes the rhythm of the breath. This is what makes yoga practice and the 4th limb of Patanjali Sutra so special, the ability to breathe and create calm in life.

In theory lectures, Sarah loved listening to guru's enlightened tales about ancient Patanjali Sutras via introduction to textbooks and self knowledge:

"A doctor would look for a problem in the physical heart and would cut it open during heart surgery. But a doctor cannot find the sickness in an emotional heart, how can he heal that?" Guru would question.

48

True. One can see with physical eyes but how does one know from sense only? Our conditioned mind always wants physical proof.

For sure, slowly, very slowly, Sarah was coming to realize that one was so much more than the physical body. Dad you shown me that. Your still, lifeless body in that side wing hospital room, reserved for those ready to leave heir body, was so full of your loving presence. Was Sarah afraid? Course not. You overheard my dear niece and I, having a right giggle at how bad you were at filling in the Christmas crossword. God bless you for filling up that room with your divine presence. And of course for Sarah to feel it.

Why yes, literally, yoga is a series of flexible postures but more so, a way of life for a healthy body mind connection. A way of loving and serving others as our God self.

Close your eyes, fall in love and stay there. Sarah did.

One morning after a particularly intense practice session, an interesting observation took place.

A beautiful, slender Russian girl, Eska, challenged the challenger by sprawling out during a theory lecture. Body language indicative of non-conformity, lack of respect and presence. The whole room filled with anticipating dread.

"My body is comfortable this way, it's staying like this,' snapped Eska.

A somber collective of downcast eyes and hearts sank. Our guru had pushed, challenged and cared for our every whim each and every present day. Never a problem, only a solution. How could she be so insensitive? As a diverse, dynamic group, we all had come a long way. Her story, her journey, her path and her karma.

Our final challenge for the day, was to hold a headstand in place for 3 minutes. Gentle, kind words and support from a German/French Shiva/Shakti, Corina, did the trick. This once fat ass was going to do it, Sirsasana, hard to do never mind bloody say. So very beautiful to feel the care and respect that had consciously grown over the past few weeks. Connected life cells from around the globe.

Bonding, softness, openness, willingness and understanding; just a few other notable descriptives that significantly shaped this pool of positive, pranic energy. Its cyclic effect could be felt by all and within it, distributed a real sense of growth and achievement. As a unit, progress was definitely in the making. You could see the satisfaction in the eyes of our teacher.

How can one ever remember all these Sanskrit names for all these postures? Plus, to know the relevant combination of asanas for chakra healing? And remember the chakra names? Sarah was used to teaching primary school children and letting the information slip right out of her head, once delivered.

Mind had other ideas. Suggested every yoga aspect needed to be a secure, known fact to become a good teacher for grown up kids. Adults do not suffer fools gladly; they would not be fooled by Sarah's usual quip…Aha…. just testing you…wink, wink...

Sarah's head was pounding so she decided to take Monkey Mind for a long, jungle trundle up to the waterfall, buried within the mountainside. She would get him to test her on the chakras wheels, so as to transfer this info into the dreaded long term memory. That would help. As a bonus though, she did remember how many there were.

Since childhood, Sarah loved counting everything and anything. She loved number, patterns, reasoning and logic. She loved trying out different calculations as a kid but always felt rushed. Has been known to spend many pastimes just counting objects, nouns, things, whatever. She simply adores spotting hidden, secret numbers, from say, book accounts, on random signs, table tops and the day to day unfolding. Bless those number angels hard at play each and every day, blessing us mere human mortals with divine intelligence.

Monkey Mind suggested stripping off and going for a little swim in the shallow end. It did look so temptingly fresh and inviting.

Sarah flipped back into pre-conditioned Sarah reality mode.

"No chance, someone might see my naked, imperfect, wobbly body!" shrieked Sarah out loud.

Sarah was not ready to do that just yet. Her path was slow and steady, she wasn't about to peel the onion layers off that quick and intense. Anyway, the water looked a bit chilly and she did not have a towel, came an internal gratifying response. Who even suggested that?

See how conditioning limits our belief system?

That is the system as we know it. It condenses and suffocates the reality of intuitively knowing, that anything and everything is possible. Of our God consciousness. Is God a separate entity from us? A separate infinite man being, portrayed to us through indoctrination? Sarah feels strongly not. How about you?

The Sarah of today has no problem in taking her clothes off (within reason; back off ego) and would not experience any feelings of shame in jumping straight into that inviting pool for a little dip, if the possibility presented itself again or if so desired. She would also find a resourceful something or somehow to dry her body on too.

Off on a tangent again, school teacher's prerogative. Life is for living and experiencing through the eyes of God, the universe, the divine intelligence, the essence, call it what you will, add a capital letter, write in in bold if that speaks to you more powerfully.

So, dear ones, our true essence and connection to every single thing in this magnificent illusion of play, once felt through direct experience, is like no other drug you will ever take. It is the drug of life! But don't take my word for it. Go and try it for yourself.

Late one evening, Eska mischievously suggested that we sneak out and go see a movie. We didn't care what was showing, we both felt a strong urge to go out and be cultured. After 6.5-hour daily yoga practice, and constant pushing through these so called 'pain barriers,' a release was very much needed. Mind wanted cake and to hear familiar sounding western words too.

Hurriedly, the evening meal was scoffed, the good intentions of the mantra and prayers delivered, the stainless steel hypoallergenic plate, Life had given us an opportunity to enjoy. Eska and I speedily made our way out of the heavy, iron doors and briskly walked down to the cinema house, which was no more that a self-made charitable shack for homeless kids, showing weekly movies and selling homemade, delicious vegetarian snacks, including pizza! Sarah's mouth began frothing at the very thought of a good gooey, carb dough base and dripping, hot melted cheese. Especially after the strict vegan purification diet.

Friendly greetings of, "Namaste...Namaste...Namaste," welcomed us on our way. The setting of the movie night could not be more unique to that which Sarah had experienced back in UK. Nor to Eska from Russia with Love.

Firstly, room was a half brick, half shack-like outbuilding at the bottom of a very dark garden that was hard to navigate in glasses.

Secondly, it was filled with candles, incense, fresh flowers, pictures of Papa G, Mooji, Osho, Maharashi and other masters scattered around the sills in ornate frames.

Thirdly, beings were lounging on top of one another in puppy piles, eyes drawn to an overhead interactive screen, sipping herb teas in quirky vessels, bodies interlocked, actually touching one another. This was a new reality. Dangerously sexy.

The western movie Sarah had seen before and enjoyed, but once the storyline started developing and the action shots became more violent. Well, Sarah observed a tightening in the chest, as if a knife had been inserted; the spoken dialogue hurt the ear drums, the pizza crust didn't taste that good either.

What she did enjoy however, was the shared intimate moments with her yogi pal Eska. How her eyes shed so much light that lit up her face like a spark when she laughed. How adorably cute the little playful kittens were that scavenged from behind the screen, timidly grateful for a small crumb. Small things like that, Sarah started taking more notice of the finer details.

As the body lay down to sleep for the evening in the surrounding comforting bright pink walls, and no, before you ask, we weren't locked out of the ashram because it was well before 9:30pm when we sneaked back in, Sarah had a realization.

The date night expectations did not come up to form. The film could not be surrendered to. That, in effect, the outing was a test, a test to self. Did she pass? Well yes, her choices had significantly improved for a higher purpose. The old Sarah had definitely been dumped somewhere.

Interesting observation.

Throughout the night, the body was experiencing physical jitters that interrupted the quality of sleep. Could it be the violence and aggressive language from the film?

During the night deep rages could be felt, but not enough to be woken up from. Note to dream diary. Is there an emerging pattern here?

"Sat Nam Northern angel," sang a beautiful kundalini fellow yogi Makri.

A fascinating, wise Danish oracle who channeled constantly from the divine, bless. How he managed any asana work with his left side muscles almost paralyzed and detached from his twisted spine, Sarah did not know. But this guy had spent many years bodybuilding; he was as strong as an ox. The divine always works in miraculous ways, once tuned it.

This guy made Sarah beam. He radiated joy and love. Never once did you hear him complain or suggest that his physical impairment altered his quality of life. This was his blessing.

Sarah poured herself her morning's hot honey lemon drink, breathed deeply, inhaling the sweetness of the brew and relaxed on the bed for several moments, to feel very present in the body before practice. Thanks to life.

Glancing one morning at her mobile phone on the side of the locker she couldn't believe her eyes...not 1 but 13 missed called from her lovely mother, pet name Doris, back in the UK. From experience this was not a phone call bringing good news. This energetically felt the same as receiving THE phone call, to confirm the passing of her dear brother a few years earlier. Peace be upon you dear brother.

Sarah knew that it was a brave decision to take your own life, using your favourite Everton jacket as a final comforter to take you onto your next karmic life.

You felt that your little boys would be ok without you? Content in the knowledge that their loving Mother would see to that. Such painful memories of a beautiful soul given the mask of an aching addict to wear.

Sarah disliked Silver Birch Trees, for a long time afterwards.

This had got to be a serious drama. And it was.

Sarah's gorgeous younger sister's husband had decided to take his life the previous evening, following a late night boozy drinkathon session. To cut a long story short, their relationship was at crisis point and in the early stages of needing space or separation. What Lil didn't envisage though, on returning to the family home to collect some odds and ends after a few days R&R with the lovely Doris, was this…The front door, wide open, with a pair of legs sticking out in the hallway, reaching from the stair banister. God bless you dear ones.

Lil was in complete shock, a mess, numb, weak, unable to articulate words over the phone, much less in person. We had not long buried our dear father, then this? Her body's natural defense mechanism had kicked in to protect her. Copious glasses of rose wine sedated her.

Immediately, being the eldest, Sarah felt the responsibility and the desire to go back home to the UK. To comfort the family, to be of assistance, to wear the mask of responsibility that she had always worn.

One can never imagine how one must feel in such circumstances. My heart goes out to all beings who experience this tragedy. On the one hand, there is a deep sense of grief and loss; on the other there is a real sense of freedom from the body and perhaps a chance of rebirth?

Sarah figures that something within demands peace and the body mind listens. If this is your body's way to go, then so be it. God decides.

Alcohol, drugs, cigarettes and medication may take you away temporarily from the suffocating daily dramas of life. In fact, any addiction will take you away from the truth. Nonetheless one will continue to experience the darkness, the trouble and un-resolved karmic patterns cropping up over and over again. Thus, dear ones, one will experience nothing but inner conflict.

Sarah should know, she has felt it. It's like being buried under the floorboards, way down low somewhere in the earth's crust. Like the dynamic Uma Thurman in Kill Bill, trapped underground in a coffin, but triumphantly knuckle-dusting her way out of the gloom. Mind over matter, focus, meditate, get up, get out. This is your PASS to GO.

However, some unfortunate beings never learn. They remain distracted from pure self love and so the karmic cycle continues; have a baby, get an extension, book an expensive holiday, buy a new house, buy a second lawn mower because you can. All these suggestions and acts of keeping the mind occupied are only a short fix. Like sticking a Band Aid plaster over an open wound, eventually it will wear off. Now if water peels the plaster off you can either stick a new one on or be fearless and allow life to heal the wound naturally. Or, take your deeper enquiry by the great big fecking horns and embrace it, hold it, nurture it, be very present with 'it' thus transforming 'it' to become your friend and ally.

"Teacher, I have to return home, there has been a serious family crisis," sobbed Sarah.

Guru, enveloped me with a mighty bear hug and Sarah could feel the warmth of his pulsating heart.

"Go up to the rooftop, sit and meditate on it, your heart will guide you to the right choice," his wisely suggested.

Sarah didn't really want to leave the course unqualified, undercooked and half-baked but felt a very strong yearning to leave. What to do? Meditate on it as guru suggested.

After a short while, of silence, of sitting in that quiet, sacred space, a suggestion to go to the Ganges came up, to place some flowers, say a short prayer and release positive energy and send lots of love back home. This was a very beautiful suggestion indeed. Sarah wanted to stay for certification, pass the written tests and experience her journey, her challenge to the end. Just as her Dad projected.

Monkey Mind had other females in his force field, so wasn't, or didn't seem to show much empathy about this situation, which was another massive test for Sarah.

So Sarah did exactly so. With support from the illuminating Goddess Tara, she sent lots and lots of love back home and had heard that the funeral arrangements were taken care of beautifully and that the whole occasion was marked with plenty of dignity and respect for a lovely, lost soul. Sarah had heard, too, that Lil had remained very strong. Bless.

Nor did Doris take my absence personally. She had suffered enormously over recent years, what with mental health problems, of psychiatric disorders, of being sectioned, of Fibromyalgia, of Agoraphobia, of experiencing anxiety and depression in various deep forms. She had her own Monkey Mind to deal with, God bless her too.

Task of the day, karma yoga. Otherwise known to man as slave labour. All yogis were given gardening tasks to fulfil, to help create a sacred, healthy vegetation plot for the ashram.

Upon foot arrival, it looked like we had walked onto a building site with tons of rubble, sectioned off with yet another pair of heavy gates. How on earth could vegetation be grown here? The land looked unhospitable and unmanageable to grow any sort of edible, organic produce on, never mind eating it as well.

Once tasks were delegated, who was moving what stones to where and removing smaller stones and weeds to what location. Guru, sat in the corner like a Johnny concrete foreman, with his ever so watchful eyes. Observing and noting every movement, every detail, every comment and barking orders every now and then.

Sarah cleared a patch of scrub land with a strapping big, young and very handsome Russian guy. We crouched down over a small area of soil and began the task of removing weeds and stones, with makeshift tools, in harmonious conversation. Albeit, in harmonious nods and smiles as this guy's English was smiley limited.

Blimey, ooops a doodle daisy, Sarah accidently snapped a lemon grass stalk, looked like a pale strand of grass anyway, so casually threw it carelessly onto the weed pile after a sniff. Guru came flying over.

"Sarah, be careful, this is bad energy, every strand of life energy in this garden is God," a non-bemused Guru firmly spoke, looking intensely into my eyes.

"Sarah take heed. Love, cherish and value everything, it is all One God source. Everything has a rightful and just so place in this life."

Imagine my face, little me, well travelled and knowledgeable little miss primary school teacher and brought up in several amazing locations including; Ireland, London, Germany, Liverpool and Manchester (cue dialect confusion).   Little Miss Know It All.... being told off...felt like throwing my toys out the pram...Little Miss No Nothing rather.

Nevertheless, knowing, feeling and experiencing this new information on a more conscious level, made Sarah question her previous existence. What had she been doing thus far? Asleep and blessed to have raised 2 gorgeous kids, that's what.

Except now, she was learning to soar, she had sprouted beautiful wings. Thank you Dad, thank you life.

Nevertheless, the wings weren't fully opened yet, they were still a bit rusty, but they could be felt and needed a little bit more TLC, that's all.

Sarah considered her reflection in a cracked piece of glass, in the garden rubbish mound. Crikey, she didn't seem to recognize herself. The full moon's equinox, had enticed her to shave half her hair off in a local barber shop above the local police station. Imagine the scene, a blond Shakti, instructing a non-English speaking male with a short back and sides Mohawk cut, to shave half her head on a number 2 blade?

As it happens, I ended up with a number 0, Britney Spears style.

Additionally, sporting a newly pierced nose ring, snugly in the left nostril! Furthermore, the body shape appeared more svelte, streamline even. A few extra wrinkles graced the brow too, but the eyes were actually smiling. Yes, really smiling. Hadn't remembered smiling or feeling this good in a long while. Sarah liked her reflection a lot.

Mid-evening revision on the rooftop terrace was always a pleasure. The small talk, the deep talk, the sharing and the connections acknowledged, over never ending herb tea top ups. The playful rooftop dramas from the little monkey rascals, who once sneaked into a bewildered yoginis room for fresh papaya! Hilarious when she screamed at the cheeky beggars to leave as they bounced around the curtain pole, as if under attack! So funny.

Mwahh, fond memories of many early evening social gatherings, whilst our teacher so tenderly, cultivated his roses. Remembering one time, when he cut a fragrant, red rose and presented me with it whilst knee deep in learning asana names, from Bhujangasana to Rajkapotasana...who would care back home about these Sanskrit names anyway? Who thought?

In the Western World it is far simpler to know them by their animal names, Cobra, King of the Pigeon, Cow or Crow pose. In fact, Sarah felt it extremely important to know and feel and learn them all.

True Yoga originates from the East, not West. Stick with the original brand. This is always best. Why would you purchase supermarket own brand beans when you can have Heinz? Come on!

Not to be forgotten either was the 5am sunrise walk up to the Shiva Lingam temple. Simply breath taking. What an intimate privilege, an honour, to witness these vibrating women in the presence of a giant lingam, throwing holy rose water over it to celebrate its blessings. This was a rare and special day trip out for almost completing our Yoga TTC.

Not to be forgotten, part of the course included a sacred 2.5-hour practice at the side of the Holy Mother, River Ganges. Each student taking diligent turns, to deliver a taught session and participate as both student and teacher. As always, our teacher observed from a distance, both our dialogue and interaction. This one time, hysterically, a passing cow trampled on the mats sending yogis running and a pack of hungry dogs stopped for a right good sniff during forward folds. Agreed, we all had trimmed down but not quite to dog bone material, just yet.

These occurrences felt far more sacred than any Sunday church service, and far richer than any vicar monotonously going on about some parable or other.

Sarah had decided that the path of spirituality was abundant in riches, God consciousness riches.

Plus, Yoga gave one the opportunity to beautifully observe how the body moved, to be felt. It is not a practice for getting out of your body, as some believe, but a real opportunity to get right in it. Nor is a practice not to be performed but observed.

Namaskar…praying hands… is the simplest asana, therefore any being can do yoga. Fed up of people saying I can't do this, I can't do that…bullshit. Yoga is a simple and utter devotion to life, consciousness, that which you are. Simples.

"Everyone, time for one more 3 minute Chakrasana wheel…hold…hold…meditate, meditate, meditate on the colour purple, Sahasrara," instructed our teacher one early morning practice.

Help me dear God, I'm in my mid 40's with a stiff back. I haven't done one of these since I was a kid way back in primary school. Mind pleaded.

When I was a young kid, there was no better feeling than doing at least 10 of these, back to back, on family day trips to the beach. Dad always admired my gymnastic ability with pride. Back in the good old childhood days.

"Lock, control, engage upper body," more broken English instructions.

"Yes that's it, it's coming, I can feel it, beautiful," smirked Monkey Mind.

"Please be quiet and mind your own business for once," Sarah hissed whilst upside down.

"Inhale, exhale, deeply down to behind the naval, send love, receive love, welcome this softness bodily feeling," cracked Monkey Mind…he was in full cheeky mode and needed a love tap.

It is at this point one feels it necessary to pay a few respects to our Guru, having myself trained as a teaching professional and therefore understanding by direct experience, of the dedication that this entails. Sarah comprehends the enormous challenge teaching brings.

More so, what this guy manages to achieve in a 28-day service to others, goes beyond love and devotion.

The teaching and learning of children is one bag, the teaching and learning of adults is a completely different kettle of fish. One has individual characters, masks, personalities, cultural differences, etiquettes, conditioning, stories, inner child conflicts etc., etc., to develop from a neutral place.

In practice, the collective consciousness reveals itself as the same essence, this our guru knows. So holding space with unconditional, parental love, both gentle yet firm manner, supports expansion and growth of the God consciousness, divine, whatever you like to call it. Sarah likes the term life.

In addition, might I add, not just for our collective and individual story but for each and every other beings journey that pass through those heavy iron doors, month in month out. Now that is devotional service.
A doctor of transforming hearts, ego minds and bodies. Firstly, by breaking them down then carefully rewiring the software, to a much clearer sense of self. Thanks to life and guidance from our beautiful guru. Aum Namah Shivaya. Om. Amen.

The joy of receiving certification was in sight, just another week then Sarah et al would be qualified yogis. It was a good job she was nearing the end of the course because Sarah had started to notice, that her concentration and focus was slipping a little bit. A lot had gone on this last month. For example, on one occasion during meal time mantra, she couldn't stop laughing her head off at the silliest of things. Not only that, but Sarah was encouraging others with her naughty infectious self. As well, our poor teacher became the butt of jokes for his cute mis-pronounced words as he would request to, 'Shhit (sit) on the shhoofa (sofa) with your sqqhooes (shoes) on the sqhhhide (side).'

Corina, you little minx you, you didn't need much encouragement either, but it was an endearing jest take from the heart space for sure. Sarah had never met her female match before, let alone a powerful German/French Shiva Goddess version, so full of vigor yet unlike Sarah, with a room full of loving products to die for. Sarah lost count of her lending sprees for soap, books, shampoo, conditioner, leave in organic apple cider vinegar spray and lymphatic drainage massage that every being should do daily.

Do you know that you have more lymphatic fluid in your body than blood? It is vital each day to massage, plus, whilst in the shower one can easily do. Simply use palm of hand or block of soap and in circular motion scrub behind knees, top of groin, inner elbow and under arm pits. Plus, ladies, don't forget to massage the breasts in the same motion too. Really vital to prevent toxic build up, keep the lymphatic fluid moving, prevents many toxic conditions building up, including the potential big C.

Oh, and another thing she taught me, if you can't put it in your mouth, then why put in on your body? So ladies and gents, pass on the deodorant spray, the chemicals will be absorbed through to the bloodstream and how does the body rid itself of these un-natural chemicals? Allergies, headaches, fever, aches, pains, whatever else manifest.

Actually, I was never aware during my sleep phase, just how much the body speaks to you. If you listen carefully enough, that is if you become conscious enough to listen, pay attention, channel the healing specifically to the chakra that needs the healing. Maybe previously, Sarah wouldn't have ended up in A&E with a lumber puncture for cluster migraine or womb lining removal for traumatic period distresses?

However, Sarah was returning to a more natural, intuitive God conscious self healing state that was once so, a skill seemingly lost in the 21st Century era.

Have you got Fibromyalgia, here take these pills, it is not Kundalini symptoms, impossible? Do you suffer from anxiety and depression? Here, take these pills. Do you have Heart problem, Diabetes, we have tablets for those too? Do you get the picture? Just sharing, once Sarah gets on her soap box, it's hard to get her off!

Congratulations and feelings of admiration and respect to you all. It was the morning of our last 2.5-hour practice. Teacher had decided to start the morning with a vomiting Kriya, a cleansing using a 2litre salty warm water bottle and fingers down the throat job. Well, I had downed a pint of lager before, so I knew how to open the gullet, hence was up for this form of cleansing.

Picture the scene; angels standing in collective anticipation in the garden rooftop, dressed head to toe in pure whites, the wind is gently blowing off the Ganges, the sun is shining high in the sky and diligent yogis are knocking back this salty phlegm in one and then projecting the contents and probably the lining of the stomach too, out over the balcony in undignified moans and belches.

Serge, the big Russian bloke was the best and first to heave, a really deep, tenor heave. He was the trigger for the rest to hurl in melodic unison. Anya, a graceful Georgian swan, lastly sang staccato.
Teacher told us to stick our fingers down our throats further. Well Sarah could do that alright. Back in her teens she had a brief spell with Bulimia. Heard about this as a form of weight loss so decided to give it a try.

Did I lose any weight? Did I have enough information about the food that we should eat?
Back in the day the internet wasn't invented. Believe it or not, everything was sourced from a book or word of mouth. Or from your best friend in the school toilets.
So no, didn't really lose weight, wasn't aware that making yourself sick on chocolate cake didn't really work, or that bread was too lumpy to bring back up. Lack of education and trial and error on my behalf. Nor would I ask the lovely Doris or Dad for their advice on the subject. You didn't back then.

Sarah found on the internet the other day, that some catwalk models soak cotton balls in milk as a food replacement. It's funny, Google can find absolutely any information these days.
Anyway, this new cleansing Kriya felt amazing afterwards, everyone felt the same with a new sense of freshness and lightness. Under teacher's instructions absolutely no sugar was to be consumed during the next 24 hours. That meant Eska, no sneaky visit to The Honey Hut for a chocolate ball and butterscotch ice cream-mind occasionally craved, well only twice during the TTC anyways.

The ashram was in full swing celebration mode, the rooms were dusted, cleaned and wiped down, the beds stripped and there was song in the air because of joy in da house. The most exhilarating moment? When our teacher handed out the certificates to rounds of applause. Sarah had done it! Physically punches the air several times! Whoop, whoop.

The old Sarah would possibly have downed a bottle of red wine and guzzled a Big Mac on such an occasion. But not this blossoming new one, who wouldn't dream of absorbing anything unsavoury like that into a leaner, cleaner, holier machine. Instead, she lovingly cleaned her room.

Even weirder, Sarah had slept soundly ever since her 'movie night terrors.'

No dreams, no thoughts, no visions, no waking up in the night with sweats or tremors or sleep paralysis. All disturbances, seemed to have mysteriously, vanished.

Daily meditation helped enormously in quieting the mind, even though at times 'it' still wanted answers. Sarah was far more more equipped now though, to take a step back, become silence and feel her truth.

The saddest moment? When our teacher had informed us that the 'bad energy' had left the building, referring to Eska, who had proved too challenging to him at times? Did she reflect back to him, something that he did not like in himself perhaps? I wondered.

Before the big, final departure back to the UK, an extra few days was spent to ponder and collect the thoughts. Time was spent sprawled out open in a beautiful, big mahogany four poster bed, drinking banana lassi, with plenty of entertainment provided by the ceiling fan, whirling round. Sarah had an obsession with ceiling fans, she just loved being hypnotized by them and could watch them for hours. Possibly, counting the rotations.

Really, it was a great opportunity to allow the science, philosophy and tradition of ancient Hatha Yoga to really sink and be digested.

Over dinner one evening, a brief encounter with an Indian Tantra teacher, who tried to activate my sacral chakra by placing his vibrating, energetic hands on my shoulders, was a tad too much. Sarah felt his desire to turn her into a loose, wanton, sexual, object, alas no, she felt too pure for that poppycock.

Intuitively, God self knew what to do in this situation, shine the light politely. Darkness will not spoil or sap your energy…. walk away my darling. Send many blessings.

Or was just just another test from source? Does darkness actually exist, if all beings are infinite slices of source?

Sarah was getting the hang of this game, yes, it felt like the Game of Life, although not a board game but a real one, so to speak, like some sort of 18-rated PlayStation game or other. Although Sarah was her own player in this game. Her very own, Miss Black.

Learnt how to make Dal too, from the Guest house elders downstairs, so I did. A feisty, cuddly mother ran the kitchen, a lovely, lovely soul. Her husband often sat, hand painting ceramic jugs in the dining area, amidst the chatter of backpackers, marveling at the fat burning properties of Ghee.

Once a being decides this path, there is an awful lot to think about. Does life just spontaneously happen?

Sarah slept for 2 days solid. She needed her strength to return to the UK, to family, disorganization and drama.

Thanks to life, to Rishikesh and all its magic! Sarah has had a blast. You have served me very well. You have been my home and welcomed me with your open beautiful arms. Your hidden gems Sarah will not disclose in her book. But she feels pretty sure those scouse lads from Liverpool, way back in the 60's, knew all about them! Love and light lads.

On the plane journey home, Sarah felt numb, like her legs had been amputated because they were extremely heavy and a ton weight. Time for a different reality now, she thought.

Why did she feel so heavy hearted? Was she already missing the humbling effects of her Indian Highlights tour? The little barefoot greetings from the Himalayan jungle kids. The free afternoons spent with the glamourous Shakti farmers, squatting for hours in the heat, sifting the tiny stones out of the corn mixture, always sharing the first chapatti with the sacred cow? Or the quiet moments spent solo practicing and mastering some tricky postures such as Garudasana…the mighty Eagle pose…high on the rocky hillside overlooking the Mother Ganges, under the glow of the early moon?

The mojo was feeling the emotion of grief as the physical body was resting the head, with a complimentary soft pillow, up against the hardness of the window shutter. Resembling Little Jack Horner who sat in the corner eating his curds and whey, who stuck in his thumb and pulled out plumb and then what?

My dear friend Monkey Mind you have served me very well too. Keeping up to speed with both my mental and physical developments. Thank you.

Sarah had started to connect with her feminine, gentle, womanly self. Her former cure for tension long stopped, that unloving 2-minute, bean flicking medication just became another part of Sarah's story.

Now Sarah felt raw, fragile, the womb had collected many years of trauma and had been holding on to it secretly for years. Incidentally, suffering many hospitalization episodes as a manifested result. Sarah would not and could not touch herself intimately, out of a new found respect for her divine femininity.

Could I let Monkey Mind do it? Help me release my Sacral Chakra blockages and heal my inner child? He seems to have become my spiritual doctor, always knowing exactly what to do and say at precisely the right beautiful time?

Over in Rishikesh, my awareness of the self's Kundalini energy grew. It began seeping its way internally through the physical body and really began to become more and more noticeable.

One quiet evening after a long meditation and before dropping off to sleep, Sarah recalls twitching and vibrating on the bed, first from the left hip, then passing through to the right. The gentle breeze coming through the shutters pulled Sarah's torso straight up out of the bed and this energy seemed to be running around like wild fire, up and down the spine, down to the jerky toes. Was she scared...No...she just observed this energy, just like Google instructed.

Google had become Sarah's number 1 friend. The more she searched and trawled about this mystical experience the more it became apparent that this was a blessing from life. To receive this activation from the dormant, sleeping serpent Shakti (coiled in the sacrum of us all), awakening to our true divine source, was an honor. No big deal then. On another occasion she remembers a mid-morning solo stroll along the Ganges, after a tasty, fresh, fruit-cocktail breakfast. When boom, it hit her, an out of body experience, like a dream but not if that makes sense? Sarah was overcome with the sense of being connected to everything around her. She had not only lost her body temporarily but had transcended it for a few trippy minutes. Sarah was the sky, the water, the cows, the people, in fact all the space around her amplified her essence. She took rest and sat down on a nearby wall to ground herself. No words but many.

The main question was; could Sarah tell her family about it? How would they react? She was under strict instructions from the understanding husband to come back energized, and get whatever was in my system out. For non-awakened beings, this is easier said than done and could sound like 'Black Magic' or 'Witch Craft' even. Sarah could understand that. So out of respect for the family's lack of knowledge and possible fear, Sarah and Monkey Mind decided to keep quiet about it. Well she didn't know what to expect on a daily basis any more. She had learnt, was learning, to let go more and go with it and trust.

"Hi, honey, I'm home," should have been the loving remark made as she strolled through the door. Instead, Sarah was feeling duty bound and angry as she un-packed her rucksack contents into the closet. Folding her yoga practice whites with much love and sentimental devotion.

It was so beautiful to see all the family, to hug them and feel their lovely presence but nothing had changed, the daily routines had been ticking over perfectly. Had Sarah even been away? The family had seemed to cope really well without her? How did she feel about her beloved husband?

With consciousness and awareness, Sarah started peeling vegetables for the obligatory Sunday Roast. Well she had been away for several weeks and felt compelled to do so. However, instead of feeling genuine love in every slice and dice, Sarah felt unhappy inside and sad. Not that she didn't love her family or anything, far from it. She just didn't resonate with this demographic beer drinking mind and meat eating culture. She felt totally out of place and in the wrong reality. Maybe this will pass, she thought.

The husband suggested returning to work and a daily routine to lighten the load, bless him, instead of 'floating around the house, listening to all that repetitive mantra crap.'

Looking back, it must have looked like odd behavior to him. Who was this woman who had returned from yet another soul searching jaunt? These were not his standard wife's characteristics anyhow?

But to Sarah this felt completely natural. She was feeling homesick for her beloved India and her softness and clarity.

On a physical and emotional level, the partnership of longer than a life sentence in jail had become strained. However, this was an understatement. More akin to 2 fireflies, rotating near each other but never getting close enough to touch. So much distance had grown between the hearts. Conversation revolved around logistics. Had the dog been fed. What was for tea and such like.

Lovers' hearts connected, need only whisper to be heard. Monkey Mind taught me that. Or they can gaze into each other eyes and need no exchange of words at all, for they share a deeper knowing.

Did our contract need to dissolve, for his spiritual growth as well as mine? Either way, temporarily or permanently, this was to be Sarah's greatest challenge.

Yet, so much fear stood at the doors of perception. Fear of security, fear of breaking up the family home, fear of this, fear of that. Fear of feckin' everything.

<u>Divine Feminine Growth</u>

One chilly morning, whilst gently easing oneself into the day with the usual piping hot, black coffee cup of deliciousness and trawling through her daily a.m. electronic housekeeping, Sarah noted an intriguing Facebook pop-up,
Mmm, most interesting, a Divine Feminine workshop led by Hridaya Yoga School sibyls from Mexico. Life had made a very good suggestion.
With some Sarah-led yoga teaching under her belt, general feedback implied that Shiva Sarah's expression, still needed work. Some female partakers noted a rough and slightly forcible, aggressive touch during alignment. What to do?

Sarah's initial classes had proved that teaching adults was indeed thought provoking and a challenge. Grown up bodies can be the worst or best critics (whichever way you look at it), unlike little bodies, who are so much more aligned and full to the brim with source energy.
Feeling rather wounded and slightly pissed off because Guru did not make us aware of this vital factor during our yoga teacher training. Did the course demand so much of his energy in deconstructing our physical body minds with such loving force, that he did not have time for this loving aspect of service to others? Or was this culturally a norm? The Indian, male way? Projected as chauvinistic? Or simply put, no pain, no gain. No gentleness exposed for soft Westerners?

Teaching yoga is akin to passing your driving test. One only really learns to drive a car after passing the test; it is subsequent experience that builds competency and skill, skill that theory tests simply can't instill.

Right, this workshop looks like a great chance to reconnect with the feminine side of herself, Sarah thought. A feminine side which, for so long, had been masked with severely short hairstyles, button down, crisp, starch shirts, A-line skirts, thick opaque tights and extremely sensible lace ups. After all, she was a good, primary school teaching role model and enjoyed looking the part.

68

Welcome back…City of Love…welcoming to all, the great city of Loverpool. Thank you once again for holding me with those great big, wide open arms of yours, she lovingly thought while making her way through the one-way system up the old dock road. The internal Sat Nav making all the wrong but right choices.

Running late, as per and conscious of the clock ticking away. Sarah decided to ask for directions at the next bus shelter insight. Life delivered. Even better than friendless verbal directions alone that often get lost in transit, a delightful male jumped in the passenger seat. He was on route to his boxing training gym not far from Sarah's venue, boss.
Noticing the yoga mats and straps on the back seat, a brief yet lovely conversation about the passions of yoga ensued then...
"Park over there laaa, it's free," Boxer Man chirped. Endearingly, all scousers sound as though they verbally sing the spoken word, like morning song, and nothing like the drone some monotonous accents sound like to the ears. Not mentioning anything at all about the Birmingham accent here, as one could be accused of being place-ist.

Just to add, Monkey Mind had also suggested that I get further in tune with 'my' feminine qualities because even 'my' lips felt hard to touch? How on earth did he always manage to make 'me' feel uncomfortable in 'my' own skin? Why was he always right too?... Reflect this?... Don't ask. Just accept.... Now who is thinking that? Has Monkey Mind a twin? Double, bubble mind provoking trouble?
Glanced at the clock, made the obligatory signature, in the obligatory register, registered a 30-minute lateness.

Offered my sincere apologies to a circle of inquisitive Goddess eyes. Then, plonked my butt down on the last remaining, plump, red cushion, which could not have been more significant in itself. On my left, a curly, blond, adorable, pixie nymph. On my right, a curvaceous, dark haired sultry Hridayan priestess who re-kindled my love affair with the Goddess Parvati immediately. Reminding one that the journey can also be romantic, a sacred romance between soul and spirit, where lovers meet, separate and come together again. No, the feminine path is not just for women, the Sufi poets followed this path all their lives. But it's one that women understand deeply, which is why so many women resonate with the sacred bond of Shiva and Parvati. For a Parvati woman, the true lover is the one who challenges her to grow, a meeting that takes place in the soul. It is hard to decide which is my favourite goddess but Parvati is right up there. A warrior, a romantic, a mother on a path of inner growth who allows life to make love to her. Hence the expression, behind every successful man lies a strong woman.

Are you a Parvati woman? Do you have these longings and desires to be like her? Sarah does/did.

Our beloved life had once again, composed Sarah's symphony of further growth by strategically placing her exactly where she had to be, to listen, to learn and to feel, in that very precise moment of time. Nothing is ever an accident. Ask David Hawkins.

I AM not sorry for this, if it feels like a missing part to you, but Sarah will not share the intimate wonders of that workshop right now. Life says no.

The only wisdom that Sarah is prepared to share with you is this:

If you feel these views resonate your being, from deep within your core. That an inner reconnection with the very beautiful, womanly self that you are then do this…Jump at the chance to experience this form of collective expansive sharing. Transformational is not the word. Donate blood or a kidney if so. In fact, Sarah believes that it should be embedded in the National Curriculum. It is that powerful for feminine attunement. Guys should have their own too, not to leave the divine masculine out either!

To conclude, precious Shakti energy communed by this intimate gathering of knowledgeable, lovely womanly consciousness, sealed feminine divineness beyond words. And not just at that moment but for all moments that followed and in such a trusting, valued, super huge way. No wonder Red Tent gatherings with Elders are so popular in other countries. No words, yet many.

As a direct result, not only did Sarah's touch consciously improve, but also an awareness of its connectivity and healing potential grew.
Not only that, Sarah's hair grew longer, as did her nails and floaty skirts. Her being became softer, gentler, more girly feminine. Furthermore, a secret guilty pleasure of owning a pair of ballet pumps, found themselves in an Amazon basket promising 'free next day delivery.'
In addition, Sarah abandoned her Itune hard core, rock and roll play list collection. Favouring heart centred chakra piano music instead.

The hedonistic screaming lyrics of yesterday, reminiscent of the days spent in a soggy Glastonbury field, pounding away in shamanic trance created by frenzied energy from some headlining Ego show or other, did not serve any more.
However, from the Sarah Story point of view, the vibe was always entertaining as recollected. However, musical integrity is always valued.

Nevertheless, the softer divine feminine transformation was fully underway. No turning back. Thanks to life.
A few evenings later, a further unexpected invitation was received, to a sober conscious gathering because sober was fast becoming the new sexy.
What an ideal opportunity to try out Sarah's newly discovered Latino, womanly moves. Chest drop, move, yoni, drop, move release, pull up, rhythm.
Did Sarah emulate this Mexican, Shakti Priestess? Sarah felt like she did and 'it' felt so deliciously good to move the body so freely in this way also.
Woaaah, consolidation of healing powers of the dance or conscious rhythmical movement. Oooops, I've given away too much already! Shh! No more talk of that.

Previously, in Sarah's story, it had been many years since she had enjoyed the delights of non dual movement with sound. Way back in the 90's she had encountered many late nights, early mornings of dancing in many legendary Northern establishments such as Quadrant Park and The Hacienda, throwing shapes alongside the likes of the king of the croon Mick Hucknall. And had immensely enjoyed the illicit early morning Blackburn raves as well. Stuck in the middle of no-where, dancing on a tractor, in a barn alongside other quirky beings bearing swimming goggles, whistles, glow sticks and happy, acid house, smiley faces.

FOMO, wasn't a term used back then but Sarah definitely experienced this, never a weekend would pass, without her direct experience with God source.

Fondly recalling that loving feeling which would arise shortly after 'dropping an E.' Giving one such powerful, strong feeling of love and connection to all. The tribe would join together in ecstatic euphoric dance; elated, bare chested full of passion, desire and self love. Wildly gyrating to 'banging tunes' as God source energy tore up and down the spine.

'Have you come up yet?' Lol. Amusing mantra of the decade.

Historically, beings have/will always experiment with drugs to deepen spiritual connection or for self healing purposes.

Did you know that Marihuana contains cannabinoids found naturally in breast milk? Believe it or not, it is similar to how pot smokers get the 'munchies,' as newborn children who are breastfed naturally obtain quantities of cannabinoids that trigger hunger and promote growth and development. It also has many other significant healing properties for other manifest sickness. If so, why illegal? Conditioning? Sheep? Pharmaceutical control? Fat cat corporate power, springs to mind.

In fact, if ingested properly, natural plant based medicines offer an assortment of life healing properties. Guru taught me that.

Coming back to the Divine Feminine workshop; did the husband notice a subtle change in my expressions? Did he notice a more feminine present woman? Did he seem to care?

He actually didn't say much, only that he preferred a fuller shape. The bigger feeder type. Feed 'em up, weigh 'em down type, like what Staffordshire bull terrier dog owners do who can't be bothered with their high doggy demands.

Sarah on the other hand, had really started enjoying her refined body mind shape.

She also started to get more Hatha Yoga class bookings, earning less in 1 week than in 1 day's primary school teaching. Did she care? No. The difference? Her money/energy that she was creating came from a different place of love.

A huge shift emerged. Life had started to happen through her, instead of to her.

Yogi students started to comment on how much they enjoyed the tunes, the mantra, a gentle, light touch and relaxed generosity of heart. This was self.

The husband's focus? Contribute more financially. The gas and electric guzzling monster in that very big, imposing Victorian beautiful house wanted its currency.

However, Sarah was intent on living a more frugal lifestyle. To sit indoors wearing a coat, hat and scarf if so. To share a lighter meal of nuts and seeds if need be. She loved birds.

Contradictory, the family? Consumed by mind. Didn't feel so. Could understand that. Bless. This was not a reality to be forced onto them.

Deep within, something felt like it was looming. It was becoming clear to cut the apron strings; they belonged to life, their own unfolding story, not to me.

Time was certainly swinging swiftly into action for this Shiva, now evidentially more Shakti, thank you Hridaya, thank you Father and thank you Mother divine goddess. For you had certainly showed me that, right there yes you, in your big, fat, juicy, open spiritual heart. Love you.

Another gift you left me in passing your physical body dear Dad? Your prized, Omega vintage watch. Which, as you know, Sarah has had made smaller, as it was a few links too big.

The Omega? A divine symbolistic noun and message confirming Sarah's truth in existence. Another wake up call. Omega and Alpha twin soul connection. Where and who is Sarah's Alpha twin? Her Lord Shiva?

Life constantly talks to us, gives us clues, but beings can be either deaf, partially deaf, hard of hearing, mute, ignorant, living in fear and mind alone or acute, sensitive, super sensitive or highly, extra super sensitive tuned in to 'it.' Get the figure of speech used here?

Monkey Mind was issued the responsibility of looking out for Sarah's Alpha twin flame. Bless him, although at times Sarah fucking HATED the bugger. Wish he would disappear more often, which to be fair, he does temporarily, in another Shakti's head. Then puff, out the blue, he reappears and we synchronistically are drawn to one another again. How are you doing love? He would ask.

What puzzles Sarah sometimes though is that he never tells me that he adores me, that he loves all the bones in my body, that he can't live without me, that I make him laugh, that I rock his world. But, alas, he is multi-dimensional and likes to live in others heads too. Sarah cannot have expectations. We are all ONE anyway he would say. He is always fucking right.

It is the age of Aquarius; Sarah can swear if she likes.

Google fact: You can trust a person who swears as they are more likely to be honest.

How does your Monkey Mind make you feel? Ask yourself then write it down. Funny what observations come up.

Note to self. The brief weekend workshop in the vibrant city of Loverpool, had given Sarah a true taste of Tantra, very true by definition, a tool for expansion. Thank you soul sisters for illuminating a deeper HEARTLOVE Connection. Chao until life allows synchronization some more. Om. Shanti.

Family Dynamics Shift

"Yes my darling, of course I will come to the inquest with you," soothed a reassuring Sarah down the phone to her baba sister, Pongo Lil, due to her nasty smelling nappies as a nipper.

A conspiracy within the deceased husband's family was brewing. Peace be upon him. Questions wanted answers. Had he intended to committed suicide? Why did he not leave a note? Did she push him over the edge? Did she do it? Guilty, guilty, guilty.
As if Lil, had put the ligature around his neck herself? She has a heart the size of China and loved that dear man for all his peculiar mannerisms. Tut, tut, Tut. As if.
Sincerely, what reality do some folk live in?
Ah yes, that was it, a drunken stupor, hazy one....Staggers out to the Bargain Booze store for another wine bottle, half lubricated already, but in dire need of more liquor to numb the inner pain, inner voice, inner conflict. Travelling rapidly now, up from the root chakra, twisting and turning its way around the internal organs, grinding and crunching momentarily due North. Suffering no fools.

Sarah knew. Sarah had felt this inner struggle. As vulnerable and as sensitive 'this' makes you feel, it is a dish best served not too hot either and without any alcoholic beverage whatsoever. Do not scoff either but observe, allow to cool, become neutral and when the temperature is pleasant. Mindfully taste. The intensity shall pass.
True, it can make you feel isolated but ignore Grace? How absurd! Crazy!

Best one can do is listen in on 'it', really listen in the silence. Meditate. You never know what will come up as we are all blessed.
For our protection from the angry mob, Sarah and Lil are seated in a side room at the courts; fond of sides rooms our family is ;-)
The waiting room is filled with over a dozen and a half furious family members gunning for revenge. Plus, the majority claim benefits so it was a good, free day out and an opportunity to get dressed up.

Sarah nips to the washroom and senses a bad energy follow her, through the door, as the door, is the door, hard and solid. In fact, an incredible surge of anger and rage projected from within that poor girl's body can be felt. Love and light darling. Tons of love and light blessings are given, as Sarah rinsed her soapy hands under the running water.

Sarah kicks off her boots as she returns to the side room, sits half lotus style on the chair and begins to meditate. Lil notices the ceiling light flickering. Sarah senses Dad's loving presence. The energy feels calm and balanced. All is well. All went well. Thank to life.
Doris, well Doris had been struggling of late. Yet another family loss to bare.
Sadly, she had forgotten to embrace getting older and the preciousness of life, even after losing so many people, one had forgotten the gift of each day.
As well, Doris had fallen into a routine of self medicating with her good, old pal John Smith and a concoction of prescribed anti depressants, anti pain this, anti pain fucking that.

On a previous occasion, when Lil and I had called in for a general visit, we found the door locked and muffled, unsavory responses coming from a presuming collapsed Doris, lying in a heap at the bottom of the stairs.
Under the circumstances, the only thing one could do, was to call the police to come and break the door down. Of course, a very charming, attractive officer arrived at the scene within a few minutes. Of course, Lil had an aqua park in her panties.

The side door was forced open; a blue light called for. Doris, sprawled across the floor in her nightwear, paraphilia strewn across the floor, eyes rolling and mumbling incoherently:
"Little Blue Duck and the Mother of Jesus would look after you in heaven my darling. Blue for a boy, pink for a girl. And the bells they will ring, they will ring.."
Doris chimed, over and over and over again.
Depression and anxiety at such depths can cause such havoc with the mind.

How did we get her out of the house? The paramedics threw a floaty, white sheet over her head, E.T style, then we briskly, wheeled her out on a stretcher.

Bear in mind, this dearly missed mother had not left the house for over 4 years. Therefore, being seen, being present and under the spell of poisonous intoxication, presented a very frightening episode to her.

Thus said, the sisters and close relatives, in particularly her lovely twin, shared unrelenting crisis trips to a variety of hospitals, to show comfort and support in her hours of need. Staying focused and present increased one's capacity to recover quickly from any difficulty presented. Or so we all desperately tried to do.

Tirelessly, keeping appointments with psychiatric teams, social services, Mental Health support workers and adhering to the subsequent long term recovery procedures that followed.

Little blue duck also paid several visits and once Sarah dropped in with him on a parachute, tumbling out of the skyline, fresh from her Indian Highlights tour, straight into the hospital secured courtyard. Om Namah Shivaya Doris, Mother Dear.

The husband? Sarah was an independent woman; she could drive to the appointments herself. She could manage everything herself. She did share a few of the witnessed goings on with him over dinner, out of his genuine concern. To exist a day in the life of a mental health patient ay? Who is/are the mental ones anyhow?

However, Sarah chose to keep him out of the drama. Through grace, by giving him his precious moments to enjoy life; to cycle at the weekends, catch up with his friends and have a few beers. The simple quiet life of a hard working family man. A good man. A great man.

The grown up children? Belonging to life and creatively getting on with living just as Sarah, the Mother, had instilled into their psyche from the tender arms of a tiny babe.

Exploring Buddafields

"If you died within the next hour, which would you choose?" Monkey Mind quizzed in a 2nd Skype call of the week. It had been a while.
"The Yoga teaching opportunity in China, or volunteering your gardening services at the Buddafields festival?" He continued.
That said. Mind made up.   Easy, no brainer. Sarah had always wanted to work a volunteer programme at a festival, now life had given her a blessed opportunity too just that. The 'job' included a 3 week camping stay to help construct a sacred meditation garden, with focal helix, within the healing fields. Guess the healing field would be full of healers then? This sure would be fun. Source felt happy and aligned.
Sarah prepared the family's favourite dish for supper and from scratch, too, Goan fish curry, before launching into her verbal patter about her next exciting adventure.

The next few days were spent sourcing a few essential camping odds and ends. For a start, the gas cylinder canisters and firelighters were in low supply.
Cannot manage without a morning's black, steaming cup of coffee from the coffee press, Sarah reflected. Was this an attachment issue?

Advertised my pending volunteering role on good old Facebook too, suggesting a lift share to cut the cost of petrol fuel. Interested in what life would attract this time, into the mysterious vortex?
Next step, sourcing flower donations to help create an ambient atmosphere in the Buddhafields garden Helix.

Being brought up in Liverpool, and rather open and cheeky with it too, this task was not difficult for Sarah. Spent a short while sifting through a list of local garden centres and decided there and then to drop in instead, speak to the Manager and request a donation. Chose a sacred number list of 3 nearby centres. The 1st and 2nd visits were fruitless or should one say flowerless. However, a paper document was needed to account for the gifting. Both centres had donated more than their fair share to local businesses already that year. So it was a firm no. The 3rd Garden centre, sacred number 3, run by a small, independent, country bumpkin bunny, who happily donated to the cause. He kindly filled my cart with a beautifully scented, random array of blooms, varying in mixture, size and colour. Such generous energy that would surely benefit such a garden of tranquility.

Although Sarah had never been to this type of festival before, her newly found, awakened status prompted her so. More so, after a recent conscious chat online, Spacetime, with her new, goddess friend Patzy. So, with the car boot loaded with heavily watered, abundance of brightly coloured, fragrant flowers, the parcel shelf holding camping items, the passenger seat holding snack provisions and highlighted UK road map showing Sarah the way to the Heart of England, off we travelled, solo, early one fresh morning. Inhaling and exhaling, the beautiful aroma of sweet smelling source along the chomping tarmac and never ending hardness of the M6, M5 South bound carriage way.

However, the 4.5-hour solo drive felt more like 30mins meditation. Hypnotic meditative driving. It's awesome, ever tried it? Interesting thing is, you can't get pulled over for it because you are completely in control, both conscious and aware of the vehicle at the same time. Class.

Internal Sat Nav…4.37 hours later…You have arrived at your destination. After only a brief detour at a local car repair shop as well, whereby a bemused mechanic passed on some more articulated directions. Sarah had missed the hidden turning several times and this guy sensed sheer utter madness…Buddhafields….lone female…car laden with flowers…Lol…

Safely and finally arriving at camp, after observing a miniscule hand painted effigy lent up against the barbed wire fence, Sarah's conditioned mind was looking for a big, bold and symbolic contrast like the in your face flag banners of the Glastonbury shindig, not too far away in the land of the Mavericks.

Informal and formal introductions were exchanged. Herb tea supped. Source felt very aligned. Smugly, Monkey Mind spotted Rupadarshians naked saunas across the field. How I wish I'd made him stay at home, the murky minded little pup.

A meditation 'whale' tent angled itself in the corner of the healing field. Geometrically, this gave Sarah a good place to pitch her tent. Triad style. Compost loos in another. Sarah's little pup tent, slap bang in the middle. Joyfully hammering in the tent pegs with ease into the soft ground, Sarah glanced up, giving her energy and attention to a passing golden haired Adonis. He looked like he had just stepped off the plane from Bryony Bay, Australia, and he had. Ladies trust me, this guy was remarkable, so in touch with his feminine side, so generous and ooozzing love and compassion. There stood a new breed. Sarah was drawn to him immediately and felt love from the outset. Sarah was a married woman and had so far remained loyal on the path of truth. God was her only lover and beloved.

Anyways, she still felt a brotherly connection to the husband at this point, in terms of deep friendship, the type you can rely on and catch up with in logistical terms. How can one connect to another living in another paradigm, questioned Sarah? How can one expect to make love to a physical body, as a release only any longer? Had been doing that for the past number of years anyway. Yet, Sarah's soul had felt destroyed, crushed, dejected and had been inhibited enough for too long.

Sarah knew that deep down, from the passing years together, that he experienced his own moments and brand of oneness. He would revel in the beauty of a bird of prey in flight. He would lovingly prepare an amazing dish, albeit enjoying a few beer bottles inside of him. And why not? He allowed my escape from normality, no questions asked. He allowed my return with the same open heart. He cared for our kids together, so very lovingly and fatherly supportive. Why then did our soul contracts end? We both knew deep down that it was time to let go. Time to move on, for new beginnings.

I stood there on several occasions feeling wide open, vulnerable, wanting to be 'seen.'

"Wake up, will you," I would scream inside.

Alas, deep down, knew that this was not going to happen and his very sentiments agreed the same.

"I'm not ready yet, the kids need a home base still," husband would softly reply.

"Let's sell the house, pay for the kids 12month rental and go exploring?" Sarah would enthuse.

The mother in law, bless her, thought I'd gone a bit cuckoo, due to all the family dramas.

Sarah, however, could not be denied her right of passage much longer, her universal calling had been summonsed. She wanted to know truth, this was always in her DNA. That same feeling that had reared its threatening head in my teens had cropped up again.

Doris, God bless her, early on had suggested that marriage and family life was the cure. Yes, it was for a long while, but now it had reared its imposing head furiously once more. God had spoken. These beautifully crazy witnessed dramas allowed conscious opening, creating God-given permission for much needed space to witness and observe and expand.

Our universe is so magnificently delicious and such a character in the dance of life. Everything and no-thing is always in correct alignment with source, exactly how it should be. Perfectly so.

"Hi, I'm Peter," drooled this charming Australian yogi, although he was originally a Northern Soul from my neck of the woods, as he saucily stepped down from a ladder.

The one and only, Peter, Saint Peter who held the golden keys to heaven.

Sarah smiled cheekily back. A sexual, very naughty thought popped into mind. Sarah sometimes, really, you are soooo very naughty!!! A northerner, smashing, he will get my northern twang. A bond was immediately formed, betwixt the 2.

"You risk an injury, leaving them pliers on there like that," winked Peter, "I'm Peter", as he carefully folded them and placed into his back pocket of his hipster cargo pants, showing just a hint of a v shape and perfectly formed abs... How Sarah loved those!
Silly me, for leaving them on the bottom rung of his ladder! Ooops.
Day 1, Buddafields Healing Garden Construction, under full swing. Sarah had slept well and felt prepared. The theme of this year's festival? Awakened Awareness. Goody, another exciting experience to unfold, believed Sarah.
"Drop that...have no expectations," Monkey Mind ordered.
"Yes, boss," came a sullen reply. Sarah wanted to experience this festival totally tout seul, on her own, and explore ones' identity and creativity au naturel. Monkey Mind was sent away on a little vacation, didn't want him keep popping up now that Hi, Peter, I'm Peter was on the scene either. Nor did I want his affectionate, subjective opinions about the healers that transcended the sacred garden that very evening. A very excited buzz filled the air, as variety of weird and wonderful folk turned up in bespoke gypsy vans, retro campers and customized pimped up touring vans. All transporting even weirder and wonderful cargo; bell tents, fairy lights, massage tables, candles, plants, dreadlocks, hunter wellies and posing magical energy. Helped too, to navigate these beautiful shamans and their wheelbarrow wielding wares around this quickly apt, awesome unfolding event.

The energy was building, one could taste it, very excitingly attractive. Sarah had never met a time traveller before, nor a Reiki Lifestyle coach, nor Quantum touch therapist. In school these adorable adults, as kids, were more than likely prescribed Ritalin to keep them unobtrusive, Sarah considered, probably placed on the autistic spectrum too. How very interesting and insightful that Sarah had so very stereotypically labelled these wonderful creative, gifted beings. Or who did?

Aren't these kids so very special and over looked by society? These are highly, super evolved beings, who chose these autistic bodies to live in. Sticking 2 fingers up to a society saying, "Fuck you, world, you are not controlling me. I'm gunna live my life exactly how I want and say exactly how I feel."

What do we do about that? We sympathize, empathize because they can't help what they are doing!

But who is having the last laugh here? God, you are so wonderfully charming.

A strapping, Hungarian, thigh-slapping Ollie, a Cumbrian fells wizard, complete with green, velvet cap and feather and I had the task of collecting woodland foliage. Wheelbarrow in hand, wellington boots and protective gloves at the ready, off we trundled. Ollie enlightening me all the way about pixie folklore. Felt like a bizarre scene out of the Hansel and Gretel story. Only Sarah was Gretel and had no breadcrumbs in her pocket.

Any removal of rocks, stones or fallen bracken had to be asked openly for permission for lending. Also, if it didn't move, don't force it, it is a part of the pixie folklore habitat. You want someone destroying your house like that? This was indeed a first for Sarah's ears. Thought he must be having a joke at my expense.

Understood children's imagination and creativity in story telling, knew the potential; to be vast, unique to all children but to cross over and apply that to adults too, who Sarah by now thought had lost the capability? Well, this was certainly another new experience.

Did it feel seriously strange, to ask permission to borrow a bunch of moss bound rocks? Of course it did, in Sarah's reality.

A fellow South African, Buddhist volunteer re affirmed Ollie's belief system too, after a quiet, intrigued mention in his ear, which kept one further pondering still.

Privately, Ollie has met the one and only 7-foot Queen of Elves, don't you know. Her skin is azure blue and she dons silver clothes. He won't mind me sharing this with you because you wont share with too many others will you?

Seriously, the 3D reality Sarah has been brought up in sucked, lacked personal growth and inhabited expansion. Although it does serve a purpose-keep little buggers sedated!

However, this 8D reality is so much more fun.

———

After a few days collective physical labour, the Sacred Garden Helix started to take shape. One of Sarah's roles was to alternate the medicine blue healing flags with the Buddha logo sign for festival seekers to appreciate. Never paid so much attention to aesthetic charm. Whizzing up a classroom display of children's work was far simpler.

Felt the initial daily check-in meeting a really vital part of a constructive start to the day. Knowing/feeling and sensing where others come/came from, in how they've slept, how they felt/feel, what is/ isn't resonating with them at that particular present moment in time. Beautiful. All establishments should start the day in this way, a very productive approach to the unfolding day.

Alongside understanding the others physical place in the world, tears may be shed too, which gives far greater light on how to approach an individual, without going into too much detail that is.

Feels like I'm going to cry. My neighbour, a long, legged Serbian redhead, has just started to play the most intoxicatingly beautiful, melodic sound from a hand organ that chimes across the field. It's pulling on my heart strings. Thank you, God. I am blessed always and in all ways.

She co-ordinally invited me to a 5 rhythms dance set, in a marquee large enough for a small aircraft, later that evening. Had Sarah felt the shamanic healing of a full blown dance set before? With shamanic bohemian free spirits? Never with pure intention only.

Oh boy, did something stir within and ignite that inner goddess fire indoors, carelessly tossing the emotional blockages right there out of the vortex, likewise in sync with other lovely beings doing the same. Joyful moans, groans, grunts and thrusts of animalistic gesticulations, awash with passion, were met on the dance floor earth. A glimpse of a juicy, pair of fleshy bollocks caught Sarah's attention, let loose from a pair of fishermen's trousers, gyrating suggestively, with another sensual much younger redhead. A very open display of loving affection going on here, they must be partners thought Sarah. Only to witness in the next breath, that they swapped places with another body, as if in a line dancing link at a country and western.

Tears started flowing down Sarah's cheeks. Her Hridayan workshop understanding had indeed, served her well.

Time for a Cacao customary, ritual nightcap, of pure yummy, velvety, nourishing deliciousness. Gorgeous to sit connected on mother earth, squatting on rustic cushions, of feeling the warmth of log fire drums, held together with simple low plinth tables offering connections and gatherings under the light of serene stars.

From the corner of the eye, Sarah spied Peter, I'm Peter. Yoga chat time. Always loved a good chat and a sharing from another fellow yogi about their discipline and beliefs. Curious bunny, Sarah.
Indeed, the splendid yoga hall tent offered many different forms of yoga throughout the day, yes even the naked variety. But Sarah has been busy painting, pouring her beautiful creative energy into the healing garden signs. And had missed the opportunity to see naked bollocks in Down Dog.

Peter, I'm Peter couldn't enthuse enough gratitude for the yoga Nidra teachers blissful, early morning a.m. practice. Sarah usually did her own at that hour but insisted on joining Peter, I'm Peter soon.

Obviously, by now Sarah had tried the really hot naked saunas but had shyly kept her panties on. However, after an early morning pee in the compost toilets, Sarah noticed a vast, array of wild flowers, naked, natural and proudly revealing their glorious essence for all to bathe in. This wonderful, natural observation gave the Sarah self a deep realization of something.
What did she do? She set herself an intention. Later that evening, she went solo to the naked saunas, whipped of her panties, then gingerly made her way from the changing room tepee to the secret trap door of the quiet, dark sauna room.
What happened next? A small swear word slipped out the mouth, after accidentally tripping over a wooden seat leg. It was rather difficult to see properly in that extremely dark hexagonal space. It was easier to feel ones' way around. For light, a few tea lights glowed, flickering several male and female, naked silhouettes jammed in like a bizarre, motionless underground tube station ride. Observing some couples, taking turns to thrash palm leaves against the skin of the back, buttocks and thighs. But that was thrillingly it.
Just then, a very long, thin, bony finger slid down my tiny frame, brushing my bottom.

85

"Is that Sarah?" inquired our resident painters voice. The very same being who had discovered the Glastonbury Green shade years earlier. Many years earlier in fact. Enjoyed telling tale to all the young girls too, Sarah detected.

Anyways, he grabbed me by the arm to pull me down in the seat next to him, very closely on the wooden bench. Sarah felt violated. Now she wasn't ageist or anything but felt this, this guy was old enough to be her Dad.

Sarah was a chatty girl, gave away far too much of her energy to folk. Time and time again life would tell her this but hell did she listen? Not much.

My darling Daddy, you would never inappropriately touch another being, would you? Even if you were a legendary Glastonbury Green sign painter. I am thinking about you right now.

"Fuck off," politely seethed through the teeth. Age of Aquarius! Lol.

Desperate to steal my energy are we? Receive a taste of my love? God may have blessed one with an agreeable, pretty face but to Sarah she never felt physically attractive. She looked in the mirror at her reflection and thought, yeah not bad. Fundamentally, Sarah felt that beauty came from within. Didn't males 'see' that about her? Her Alpha/Shiva soul mate will/would.

Anyone seen a Louise from Scotland? The last few days got sick to death of asking this question. My Facebook advert for a car/passenger/lift share received a response from a lively Glaswegian called Louise. Can't be many at the festival Sarah thought. Her search for her travelling companion continued.

One morning, after a duty bound check in and a guided group meditation on loving kindness, Sarah was sent to the kitchen tent to offer her service there. There were a few prep chefs down and they needed help with prepping to feed the 5 thousand.

No problem, off she twirled through the bric-a-brac assortment of organic chai tea stalls, smoothie makers, second hand ethnic hippy woolen jumpers, hula hoop demonstrators, unicycle wheelers, males hugging and crying openly in painted toe nails. Bliss.

She walked into the singing nun's kitchen, and was met by angels congregated around a big prep table like a conveyor belt, churning out salads and chick peas rice savouries. Sarah was to be seated round the corner near the open tap, to rinse, clean and toss 700 or so lettuce leaves. She was met by a pale skinned, buxom, curly haired redhead, who's carefully perched ass balanced juicily on a miniscule elf stool, with soft hands busily, yet gently, keeping up to speed with the task at hand.

"Hi, I'm Sarah, at your service," smiled me.

"Hi, I'm Louise, grab a stool next to mine, I'll show you what to do," kindly smiled a fun loving Glaswegian accent ever heard.

Sarah and Louise had found each other, the Facebook lift share home. Hilarious. We must be in the universal flow of the vortex. Sarah felt aligned. This was a very good sign. Search over. So we chatted and laughed our way through those lettuce leaves in no time at all. Hardly coming up for air, in between fits of giggles and unapologetic howls of laughter.

"Have you met my younger sister Clara yet?" Louise enquired. "She has been serving up the breakfasts, aye, in the kitchen daily?"

No Sarah hadn't but, later that evening in the dance tent, while throwing out some loose shapes, BOOM, Sarah and Clara connected and by George did they both instantly feel it. A surefire soul sister reunion. Magnetized, they both instantaneously felt the same and years and years of catch up quickly fell out of the mouths. Intimate sex talk followed with appreciative breast fondling during a naked sauna. Yes, lots of juicy curve touching in the underground humid darkness followed by heavenly, chocolate shower gel showers, back rubbing exchanges, lovingly so, under the gazing night sky littered with twinkling stars.

'Look at the stars, look how they shine for you, and all the things you do, they are all yellow,' echoed the chorus. From the bare bum brigade too, hovering over the log fire, trying keep their bits warm. Laughing hysterically at Nadia, a Punk Rock Shiatsu Empress, by almost singeing her minge on the flickering flames as she joined in the song chorus, adding some right strong Yorkshire tones to the mix.

How did Clara manifest a tray of fresh pineapple and strawberries, to play a saucy eating game with? The rule insisted was you couldn't help yourself to the fruit, someone had to take it off the tray and put it in your mouth for you to temptingly savour. Hilarious and simply slippery, juicily wonderful. The dark had become Sarah's friend some more.

Before mind conjures up wicked bisexual thoughts about our friendship, let me share this. The energy created was of pure soul sister essence, innocent, girly and sooo much inoffensive fun, without any expectations hanging around the place. Blissful.

The stipulation of the festival, no alcohol or drugs, only celebrating life source highs via collective Puja chanting and natural elements, set the scene for this purity of intention and high energetical blessedness for all beings from the North to the South, East to the West, as above and so below, including tiny creatures great and small.

Tattoo Nadia, a real life punk rock love goddess Tara in disguise, had given one's body an earlier Shiatsu half hour session, re-activating the delicious Kundalini, sending currents of ecstasy shooting straight up the inside leg, which she commented on rather matter of factly. It dangerously took the breath away and sublimating the energy took a real focus. Very surprised too, to learn of her sexual abstinence, given her punk rock, glamour puss status. What a rock lady.

Typical of Sarah during another harmonious guided group meditation, her re-activated kundalini unexpectedly kicked in some more. Sarah observed that it seemed to awaken more keenly around souls who resonate with Sarah's own. Who could resist being wedged between the charms of a long legged desirable redheaded nymph and the contrast of an equally stunning, punk rock chick on the other? Felt that strong magnet, uncontrollable jerky pull, vibrating from within and transmitting outwards from close proximity.

It is rather an amusing physical bodily function to be aware of, thou ignorance is kind. Except in this case, Sarah held the delicate hands of both supporting Shakti goddesses for them to soak up and enjoy.

Sarah's instrumental dynamics to a Sexual Therapy workshop with the impish but equally sweet silver fox, Jake, bless him for his worship and adoration of the female form in all her wanting, desirable, glory. Drew a bigger crowd into the tent we did too. He shared his knowledge of the sacred Daoism practices of the East, much the amusement of the younger generation, who initially sat ears open, mouths closed, but absorbing and feeding on this dear, sweet, valuable information. Sarah's contribution was light hearted lovingness ingredients.

Sarah laughed her head off, too, at his flippant Freudian slip of the tongue about women on women, a truly innocent gaffe, when sharing the importance of secreting saliva during lovemaking or foreplay so as to share DNA on a cellular level and therefore connect much deeper. Adding, the importance of rubbing the said liquid around the breasts and vaginal lips for an increase in electro magnetic, cellular deeper heart connectivity, Doaist tantric style.

Similarly, the input from 3 lovely teen girls, full of the curious wonders of early doors university life, literally took Jake's eyes out on stalks, when consolidating their unanimous agreement on porn masturbation, which is better to watch if it includes women, rather than men or heterosexual couples. Well, this was also fresh news to Sarah, who found the use of porn disturbing and offensive, not what intimate lovemaking was about to her anyway.

Of course, Sarah understands on many levels why beings chose to opt for this means of gratification, but sincerely, the path of consciousness, the I Am presence, the essence, will only serve one a tantric, loving open heart course.

For a brief moment, I felt a sense of wishing that my own daughter was present right there and then in that workshop, too, so that she would come to know of her mother's genuine sensitivity, concern and humour in examining such delicate, important issues. To talk to me about her own feelings, about her own womanly loveliness. Listening to her Mother holding sacred space, with joy in the eyes and the heart.

Many released a lot that afternoon, beings left that marquee with a shared sense of an awakened intent to honor the body more as a sacred vessel of source. Sarah was a happy bunny and had always fancied herself as a Mrs. Focker ditsy sexual therapist type of woman. One has to love Barbara Streisand in that mother Focker movie!

Sarah over heard a young boy squeal, "Daddy, what that lady doing upside down?" Daddy was busy putting on the BBQ for their vegan sausage breakfast.

Sarah was mid way through her mornings yoga practice in full shoulder stand cycling the legs mode, in harmony with the glorious a.m. British summertime mode. The birds were tweeting, the grass is damp and feels lush and there is that countryside smell in the air that one cannot jar, it's pure, clean indescribable form. One cannot explain it rightly so either because it is THAT good, one has to feel it type of smell.

"Hello, my darling, would you like a chai tea," interrupted Lulu, the pale skinned, long legged red head.

Sarah almost choked.

"I have no acupuncture appointments for the next 30-mins, care to join me?"

"Actually, I have a splinter in my foot that I need help getting out, maybe a needle of yours will help?" Sarah politely asked.

"Sure, come over in a few minutes, I'll get all my things prepared." She huskily replied.

When I say come over, I literally mean a few steps to the right. Another geometrical triangular, relevant universal gathering. For in the 3 corners of this sacred shape formation; Hi I'm Peter, Peter, Lulu long legs and Sarah short. Very interesting combination.

Lulu had an amazing 6foot slender frame, milky skin, a sensual raspy voice and thick reddish, rich curls which fell down weigh down past her shoulders. She was a natural redhead too, how did Sarah know?

During our chai girly chit chat, she kept flicking her short floral skirt up to reveal a glorious un manicured lady garden, peeping out over her black, silky panties. She looked deliciously beautiful.

Us women are so blessed to have such beautiful anatomy, Sarah thought, God what a magnificent creator, as she lay in the lap of her latest new connection, while she held the foot tenderly, whilst trying to get the offending object out with her tiny acupuncture pins.

By the magical power of synchronicity, who pulls the canvas door back of the bell tent and enters casually ruffling his damp, freshly showered hair, to see what's occurring?

He had had a tough morning lovingly repairing the pond structure in the garden space. Typical of British weather, the previous evenings downpour had destroyed some of its assembly, so he had spent the morning carefully restoring its Zen.

Amusingly, the downpour encouraged many organic beings to ditch their clothes and wash with the organic soaps, right there out on the lawn. Sarah too, Dr. Bronner's lavender style, her favourite. Cue life, well done, to shorten the queues for the outdoor showers which were getting unnecessarily longer. Adding a new definition to outdoor power showering?

Peter, I'm Peter, decided to lean in and gently take hold of my foot, for a closer inspection. What had Sarah manifested? I can swear this was not my doing, really it wasn't.

Anyway, as I lay back, looking up at these 2 gorgeous souls softly examining my foot, squeezing gently to get the splinter out, Sarah sensed the chemistry. This was an unusual expression for me, which didn't feel sexual in nature at all, only loving?

Sarah could sense that Lulu was carrying a lot of frustrated sexual energy within the body. It wasn't difficult to guess that her devotional husband's subservient nature made her desire more. He worshipped the ground she walked on, who could blame him, but this female body had an insatiable yearning for deeper connectivity, Sarah felt.

"Fancy joining a yoga nidra class in the morning, you 2 lovelies," Peter, I'm Peter oozed. Adding, "It made me cry this morning, so tugged on the sensitive heart strings."

During own solo practice Sarah could hear the harmonizing romance of a sweet sounding accordion playing, casting an eerie essence like a quivering fisherman's net. It had certainly pricked up one's ears and attention.

We both had a little free time in the morning as the garden structure was complete, a minimal daily task of titivation kept hands busy for a short while only. We both accepted the invitation kindly.

Spent the remainder of the sunny day, wandering around the festival, lazily observing and absorbing this wonderful creative, peaceful loving community.

The children's field was something else, very imaginative and organic, far better than anyone that I have ever had the opportunity of attending in previous years, with 2 small nippers. Trust me, I have visited a few to inspire the kids over the decades for sure. All in the line of mother duty. :-)

Mulling around, observed doting Dads cross-legged in heartcircles, in small funky bijou bell tents, nursing babes in slings, loudly singing nursery rhymes alongside workshop tambourine tapping planners. Gorgeous to observe/absorb such tenderness.

Even for older kids, there were a lot of fun and challenging, original, thought provoking activities on offer, too; fun obstacle courses, hula hoop challenges and handi-craft hand eye co-ordination practical fun chances. And not a place to dump your kids off at either, so one can go off and swig a few more tins of cider. Why does one take kids to a festival to consume alcohol around them? Strange.

Dear Buddhafields, your sentiment is so loving, you certainly excel on good old fashioned honest tradition and bless these upon puritan Buddhist values.

In addition, it was a real blessing to observe a 2.2 nuclear family enjoying wandering around the site, laughing and fooling around in only their birthday suits, wellies and huge smiles. Quite rightly beautifully so too.

Sad thing is that one could just envisage a Facebook thread or similar forum in light of these guiltless antics, launching an attack citing the civil rights of the child per se. Claiming child protection rights while an opposing lovely other half, would embrace the freedom and the fearlessness of the family per se.

Censorship nakedness at Buddhafields? Ridiculous.

The reality of varying paradigms of folk obvious, on the one hand, sexually deviant, on the other, liberating and healthy.

Sarah knew which camp she stood in. She fully admired and respected this open family, who lived outside the box, yet the box does not exist. Monkey Mind created it.

92

Early sunrise, Sarah's travel mug was filled with rich, hot, smoky goodness. Savouring the flavor as it slipped down the throat while watching the sun rise over the magnificent helix. How captivating the view was; the medicine blue flags danced in the soft breeze and the suns rays, heightening the vibrancy of the different coloured petals and plants on show.

Sarah casually walked over to the yoga nidra class. Already at least 50 bodies lay down like itsy sardines in tins, packed in tight rows under natty colored blankets. A strong mixture of energies hung in the air. Sarah felt excited and allured, spotted Lulu and Peter, I'm Peter in the middle row, with a little space saved especially for a wee one, Malcolm in the middle me.

Upon laying down, getting the self comfy, could feel a deep rumbling from the solar plexus area. Sarah pulled the red chenille knitted blanket up a little further, to cover her shoulders. That's it, get yourself snuggled in, relax, let go and drop any expectations...drop it. That's a good girl.

The Kirtan started playing, beings quietened down in earnest, strong accordion sounds filled the air whilst an equally beautiful mantra left gurus Scottish mouth so very sweetly, sending Sarah et al deeper and deeper into bliss. Only briefly recalling a brief flip out of sage role, to sharply inform late arrivals:

"Squeeze in quickly, lets be 'aving 'y'all lie dawn, aye." Before returning back to angelic guru hush tones and sending beings out into the cosmos some more.

It did not take long before Sarah was unable to maintain any physical body control. Even though deep in bliss, it felt as though the body was being pulled apart horizontally, both from the inside and outside, simultaneously to both these lovely souls lying either side on the tarp. The Shakti energy wanted to rip the chest open and tear the throat chakra apart. Sarah tried to sublimate, but the energy was getting too intense, the more she tried any pranayama, the deeper and more penetrating the currents grew. Shakti was relentless.

Sarah did not identify with the phenomenon, nor get overwhelmed by it, nor think she was special, a chosen one. She just observed it, felt gratitude and then 'dropped it.'

Peter, I'm Peer could sense my increased vulnerability. It was an unstoppable force. Reassuringly, Peter, I'm Peter grabbed my hand from under the blanket, aware that I started to moan silently now too, and began stroking my hand whilst Lulu stroked my shoulders tenderly. Fuck.

The guided meditation part was nearly done so he scooped me up, flipped my legs into lotus position, then enveloped the body with his lithe, muscular frame from behind, straddling his legs around mine to help the grounding. Sarah was in another reality but remembers him vividly stroking her hair while whispering beautiful Hari Om Sat Nam's down the ear canal and keeping the blanket, snugly around the torso for warmth.

This felt very good but also no good, another double-entendre. Fuck. Sarah felt close to full body orgasmic explosion. The yogis filtered out in a dreamy haze. Oblivious.

Unable to concentrate on the breath work properly and possibly sensing my increased arousal, Peter, I'm Peter, raised me up in his arms and carried me outside on the lawn, face down, for fresh air, placing a caring hand on the centre of my spine, before launching himself physically onto of me, smothering my petite feminine entirely with his masculine.

Peter, I'm Peter spied a concerned Lulu sauntering over with a playful little finger curled and playful baby blue eyes. Lulu would not miss out on the fun and plopped her full 6ft milky frame, straight on top of Peter, I'm Peter, and began rubbing the soles of Sarah's tiny feet. All loving soaking up all that sizzling Shakti energy like gyrating, orgasmic butterflies.

After a long while, the dogs on heat snapped apart as if someone had thrown a cold bucket of water over them.

"Right little miss, time for a feed, let's eat, I'm starving!" Prompted the lovely Peter, I'm Peter whilst yanking me up off the ground by the arm.

Looking straight into those gorgeous green eyes of his, all I could mutter was, "Thank you."

We skipped over to the breakfast hall, in silence. Felt so grateful, right then, for having such understanding loving connections who fully supported my being through this unfolding. I can't imagine how I'd feel if that kicked off at home. Well actually once, it did, but I explained it away as a migraine which needed a few day rest in bed to recover from.

Do I recall a little ménage a trois foible in the woods? Entered via by a secret password? Under a wooded night sky with protective Peter, I'm Peter's tarp?

"Good morning darling," Sarah smiled, "Did you get to the yoga nidra session this morning, wasn't it uplifting?"

"Aye, but did you see the energy fuck going on outside?" laughed Clara, "Fuck, me I wish I was in that!" She roared as she dolloped a ladle full of scots oats into my bowl.

"It was me at the bottom," I shyly replied.

"Aye, fuck me, I should a known," she laughed some more and lovingly flicked me on the arm with a tea-towel in jest.

"So I'll be seeing ye tonight then? Fancy a chai tea and a Journey of Self workshop in the Dome, 7:30pm?'

"Aye, lets see what unfolds," Sarah responded in her worst Scottish accent.

Returning to her little pup tent for a little Savasana, to contemplate the crazy mornings antics. Sarah noted 3 tent pegs missing from her outer tent, a favourite t-shirt and OM earrings from inside the Hunter wellies were missing. Weird. Searched high and low in the tidy but compact space. No signs anywhere.

Coincidentally, Ollie passed by and I asked him about said missing items?

With that, he physically bent down into the tent, physically got hold of a knee high apparent object and then I actually witnessed him gently release this knee high object back into the pond's Helix.

Ollie began to explain that I had been mischievously pranked by woodland pixies. It was notorious round here for it, in Somerset apparently?

Also, if one ever gets lost in a field in these parts of the woods, simply take your jacket off, turn it inside out and voila, in Maverick record time, you'll instantly recognize where you are. Never did find said items though?

In compensation, Ollie wanted to give me a hug. He had recently undergone a hugging workshop and wanted a model. Sarah had never hugged longer than 20secs before, the time it takes to increase the love hug oxytocin levels. The feel hug factor.

This big man used his big paws to manipulate my body into place, left side to corresponding left side heart connection, relax the feet, soften the chest, gently lay the head on the shoulder (or chest if your blessed with short legs like me). Then synchronize the breath, in unison to circulate the energy. I could feel his lingam tingling slightly. This seemed more of an energy fuck hug to Sarah.

However, really it was just another beautiful moment to experience being held, being seen by a very gentle, loving male presence.

Sarah felt really heavy waking up one morning. She felt a sharp twinge running down her lower lumber spine and into the tops of her legs. The usual mornings caffeine hit did not inject me with the poison like it usually did.

Sarah felt the cold and damp from outside the sleeping bag. Felt the sides of the tent, it must have been raining hard in the night, one side had collapsed onto the inner causing a damp patch. The dampness seemingly seeping into my bones even though insulated deeply in my -10 womb, quilted bag complete with: buff, beanie hat, base layer, fleece, socks, thermal long johns camouflage jacket and grandma's hand knitted woolen jumper for warmth. Still could not feel/get warm.

Christmas cracker joke: Heard about the guy who went shopping for a pair of camouflage trousers?

He couldn't see any!

Unzipped the tent to step outside and investigate the damage, struggled to put on my boots without getting the feet wet from the soggy ground. The land's quite boggy in the deep South.

Lo and behold, no wonder the inner and outer tent had touched during the night's downpour, more tents pegs were missing!

"Pixies!" Sarah smirked.

Sarah fell back into her cocoon and stared up at the tent roof blankly. Fondly remembering the evenings Puja deeply resonating with the soul. Feeling the power and passionate joy of the repeating mantras and the powers of intention, drumming over and over again, as a Fibonacci sacred wheel of intent. Recalled feeling woozy, light headed, drunk like, smiley and extremely joyous as the whole 'whale' Buddhist temple was a blaze with beautiful, singing and rejoicing baby calves.

Then it hit her. Well someone did, during an afternoon of acro yoga. In the form of a strapping 160 kg brick, power house Shakti Maria. Sarah was the holder, Maria was flier and a goal keeper. Need I say more?

Imagine that…A fragile 160cm, balancing a hefty 178cm giant with the soles, feet and hands only. Sarah, where did that God-given Superman strength come from? Rhetorical question answered, lol.

Even funnier, Louise, who I had been looking for all week, good job her name wasn't Linda, observed Clara and I arguing like crazy as who would do what between them in their acro yoga trial. Both dominant Shiva persona's arguing to be the holders in charge. Did we end up doing it? No, neither of would back down or was in the least aware of the comedy of the situation to others. What was the theme of the festival called again? Ah yes, Awakened Awareness.

However, juicy buxom Louise found the moment most comical. Standing there roaring, an epiphany of radiating gorgeousness, with her soft, pinky nipples peeping out from behind her dark, silky green, low cut gown that skimmed her curvaceous hips and extenuated her milky, porcelain skin, curly thick locks and dazzling blue eyes. Most alluring to the masculine energy, in fact magnetizing in aura, in glowing etheric sensual body and in passive, magnetic field. Did she realize her own power?

Another eye opening awakening experience occurred for Sarah. Was it Paganism or Buddhist in principle nature or a combination? One couldn't be sure. Felt very confused.com.

The earth, fire, wind and water elements were suggestively positive in 4 corners of the garden 'world.' Dressed appropriately in symbolic colours to represent the corresponding elements; blue, gold, yellow and green, face painted to the hilt and all, like subservient ninja power rangers. Sarah thought a purple Tinky Winky Teletubby was needed as un-disclosed 5th element though.

Duty bound, at least a 100 lovely beings linked hands, with the left to receive, right to give, to forge together a sacred wheel procession, swirling around a centralized giant symbolic monument, chanting collective thanks to life. As above and so below, thanking beings from the North, beings from the South, the West and the East.

Suddenly, within a flash, a little chubby autistic boy, around 9 years tall, ran amok amongst bewildered face participants and laughed very loudly too. Who incidentally, were by now circling closer and closer to each other, bodies getting nearer and nearer to meeting point. Chants becoming louder and louder as if to phase out this boy's performance.

Could his embarrassed mother catch him? No, he kept slipping out of her grasp and ran further into the tightly knit congregation.

Sheer brilliance, what that little kid's divine self did, exactly reflecting what Sarah felt at the time too but didn't have the audacity to do so.

Direct lesson learnt? That life should not be taken so seriously, come on!

Time for a much needed release, after what seemed like an eternity, mashing up thousands of chick peas for a veggie Dal to feed a very hungry 5 thousand crew.

Felt like a real life Jack and the Beanstalk, living in a giant's world with huge over- sized masher, the entire length of the body, hammering away furiously in a tin bath to prep the peas. One could have easily rolled the trousers up, jumped right in barefoot and proper gone for it hell for leather. Squiggling that their chickpea gooeyness right out between the toes and probably doing a quicker job. Great cathartic energy release probably, too.

After a lovely dinner on the lawn, the vibe attracts your tribe girl troop headed off for a 5-Rhythm Dance. For those of you who have never experienced this unique type of healing before, it goes like thus:

DJ/Healer/Teacher/? Holds sacred sensitive space, orchestrating body movement to carefully selected sounds, via head set and microphone MCing over tunes. Therefore, allowing the physical body to move in whichever way comes up, paying respect to the 7 known chakras in turn.... For example, the sacral chakra, the Swadhisthana is a water element, which can and does make beings open up and cry, depending on internal/external 'blockages.'

Furthermore, each energetical chakra has its own magical element and release.

So yeah, the Shakti tribe is all going for it, letting loose on the dance floor, spreading out from our initial tight Shakti circle formation, until one can barely catch sight of any being, yet lost and very aware, in one's own bodily responses.

When suddenly, the tempo changes and binaural heart chakra beats for love start getting wildly erotic, imploding the ear drums while garments of clothes started flying through the air, forcing gyrating, sweaty bodies to contort; writhing in and out of happy cat-sad cat, frantically, animalistically with huge sexual overtones.

At that point, the 'me' felt done. 'My' heart centre felt open enough, this dance no longer resonated with me so Sarah left; Savasana in your lovely pup tent is waiting for you. Later guys. Love you.

Reflecting on the evenings debauchery, whilst sauntering dreamily en route to my pup hotel, passing cosy chai tea tents, cosy log fire burners and intimate chit chats going on. Feeling completely exhausted, but happy at the same time.

Unexpectedly, who stepped into my vortex? My universal flow? The one and only and completely charming, Worzel Gummage cross Aunt Sally cross Liam Gallagher Mancunian, totally egoless, full of swag and completely hilarious being that was… Les. Buddafields finest hairy, legged, 10 o'clock shadow, steward. Not as if Buddhafields really needs stewarding because of aggressive, drug related incidents, more like peaceful diversion of souls.

Anyway, in her broadest deepest Manchester animated accent she started telling Sarah a goodnight tale of further pixie misbehavior. Talk of switched signposts on leaving the Buddhafields bubble for the chocolate contraband run for the workers. Of missing socks and disappearing tabards. Sarah couldn't help laughing her head off. Not at her but with her and her endearing floppy, silky, pink, bow hat, that she had turned back to front, so the girly bow couldn't be seen from the front angle. So she's trying to be all macho and serious in telling the tale, complete with female Shakti bow hat, short back and sides crew cut, mid length track suit bottoms, socks and sandals while rocking an animated Liam Gallagher. We both cracked up laughing. Goodnight darling. Oh the sweet wonders of this charming life.

With goodnight fondness, observed the creative hand painted signs that I had so fondly poured beautiful energy into, hardy enough to with standing any damage from the recent downpours. Still looked amazingly fresh and robust even though only used silk emulsion and poster paints, the non-waterproof variety! The blessed life eh!

On Sarah's last evening, she dissembled her little pup tent, gathered her belongings and donated her flower trays, which were still gloriously in full bloom, to a local Hospice.

Lulu and her generous hubby, had kindly offered their tent to kip in as an early a.m. departure Northbound loomed. Sarah said a fond farewell to the late night naked saunas and log fire musical gatherings.

Felt at ease in her family tent, littered with the joyful, musings of an impressive, little boy. Felt our energy fuck, had given Lulu a fresh new way of being. Sensed a new acceptance? Understanding? Forgiveness? Joyfullness? Was this moment indeed enough satiety, to keep her insatiable Shakti drive going for now. Enough to console her conscious man?

Sarah did not manifest this desire but merely questioned life if the lovely, Peter, I'm Peter would drop into the universal flow of things for a cheeky hug? Embrace?

Remembering with the fondness, the time he asked me, "Have you been abused?"

During an amazing workshop exploring the yogi self.

"Er, no, why?" Self replied.

Consciousness interjected:

Yes, you have on a soul level that you have ignored. For many years you have made love with your physical body only. But now life has blessed you, you are awake to a different state of consciousness, your former reality will not suffice one any more.

A deeper soul level contract will only be accepted by Sarah now, for her expansion and growth and self of the I am presence.

Deep in the pit of the stomach, those words were felt with such clarity.

How does one make sacred love to a female body? Why do Western men seem to know how to ego fuck only? However, this is not their fault.

Slight overemphasis but essentially; pump, pump, pump, ejaculate, lose semen, lose power, roll over and then fall to sleep. A divine conscious male sympathetic to the needs of a divine feminine, certainly wouldn't. Sarah had learnt this.

Divine Goddesses? Does this sound familiar to you too? Pull nightdress down, stare at ceiling, feel wetness dripping down the thighs, strategically tiptoe to bathroom, so as not to drip this vital life force energy on the freshly, hoovered carpets?

Now then, gorgeousness, we don't want to start cleaning this sticky goo up at this hour now do we?

Lie back in bed, eventually drift back off to sleep after planning the next day's food menu, forgetting all about numbness, too much to do next day, must sleep.

Question, this weird but true fact: If a man produces enough sperm in a day to replace the worlds population in 6 months, how much creative power is the Western man leaking unnecessarily from his body upon ejaculation then? Monkey Mind answers…. "Freaking tons!" Yes, he has temporarily returned. Quiet without him wasn't it?

The piercing sound of a 6am alarm call, startled Sarah out of slumber. No late night call from Peter, I'm Peter then. Ah well, no worries, all is well, all is perfectly so.

Lugged the remaining camping gear up to the car park, gave patrolling Les a super sized bon voyage kiss-cuddle. How on earth those Indian women, managed 25kg on their heads without flinching, I didn't know. Sarah's anatomy was carrying similar and was bogged down and struggling, very much so.

Louise, you raven haired, mystical Scots goddess you, hop in, dump your junk in my trunk. My Facebook lift share and I, would share petrol costs as far as sunny Manchester.

Quick to fathom why life had intended our divine connection, during our 4.5-hour magical mystery ride up North together. En route, we shared pleasant tears as they rolled down our stained cheeks. The power of spoken words, so very influential, as reminded by the Wake Up tune by Marla Maples and played for the 10th time in a row. Makes such a huge difference the place in which mind operates from, comes from, from that still place of intention. I will, I might, I never, reframe…. I am, I will… blah, blah, blah. Feel the difference? The power, the drive of source energy? Beautiful.

What else was shared?

That she had walked out on her high profile charity role. Why? Infuriated by the lack of empathy, from a previous African trip. Lou was more concerned about an African woman's plight, who had suffered devastating tragedy through conflict. She was not only sick from dehydration and lack of sanitation, but her family had been torn apart. The powers that be were more concerned with the US American actress who was waiting to interview the victim; standing anxiously, ready and waiting to get the job done and recorded on camera. A polished beacon of made-up, airbrushed perfectionism.

Lou was adamant in allowing this woman to continue her story, by holding her gently, in her delicate and sensitive hands. However, the camera crew and actress were insistent and impatient. Lou quit. There and then. Wow. Lou has a generous, open, juicy heart.

Dive in, dare you?

Perhaps one will lose the pennies but gain one's soul, oneness and freedom.

Harmonious tears rolled down the cheeks as we weaved cautiously in and out of lanes of heavy traffic. Witnessing the breath, the heart space, other car engines and over head passing birds of prey. All moving, moving this way and that, forwards, backwards, sideways or not? Observed through this meditative driving that: 'Everything is motion and motion is life.' Good shout out, Mr. Neale Donaldson Walsh.

The son, the boy, asked me how I meditated whilst driving. Given once, during an agreed taxi ride, that I appeared to magically shorten a drive to half it's stint, which during early morning Manchester rush hour traffic, can take minimum of 90mins ETA. The awesome power of meditation and the powerful illusion of time! Needless to say, the boy was on time for his work commitments. No words, many words. Thank you life.

Glaswegian Goddess Louise and Sarah bade their farewells over an organic, juice smoothie in a trendy Manchester vegan bar. Ready for the next part of our stories to unfold.

Lunch suit guys choked openly over their feta cheese ciabattas, in awe of the female, girl on girl, farewell exchanges going on. Oxytocin loved up, we had both done the hugging workshop you know and didn't feel the need to explain.

Laters, my beautiful soul sister.

A repeated pattern emerged on walking through the front door. Cabin fever syndrome kicked in, no sooner as I had unpacked my yoga Ali baba comfy's away.

Oh dear wasn't Sarah satisfied this time? Hadn't she learnt from experience enough to appreciate the life lessons from this little jaunt?

The 4-bedroom spacious semi detached Victorian home offered more than enough for any wife who desired it all. The beautiful home, the beautiful, amazing husband, the adoring kids. So why desire more, greedy, selfish Sarah?

A surprise change of events had moved the boy's teenage girlfriend into the home. Bless. She had settled in very nicely, too, and integrated well as part of the family. Now though, 2 sets of reflecting mirrors were in da house. Sarah's head felt screwy.

The boy and GF; hippy, creative, playful, musical, scruffy, untidy, arty, adventurous, out door loving and tactile foodie puppies.

The girl and BF; organized, tidy, clean, meticulous, structured, orderly, manicured, nature loving and passionate foodie bunnies. All so very loving, yet very different reflecting mirrors.

What type of mirror did hubby and Sarah reflect? Uncertain, since the strange twist of dynamics that were to present themselves over recent years? Soul companions? Life companions? Deep friends? Hoped so.

Sarah is certainly not advocating her spiritual path is superior or greater than those aforementioned. Far from it. Each is source and walking home their own perfectly formed way for their own soul's evolution.

Sarah was also very careful not to sound like a bossy, patronizing cow, full of spiritual loving intentions, but after her latest shared direct experiences in the gorgeous Buddhafields bubble, who could not want to burst with joy and share?

Sarah kept relatively tight lipped and meditated in the darkness with her friend candlelight, occasionally skyping a growing number of like minded beings from around the Interglobe. To unleash, to question the hearts desires, perceived by the perceiver, observed by the observer. I was not mad. I was home within a family of familiarity.

Felt it hard to arrive home in the physical sense though, to land properly once again, not to mention feeling restricted by the clothes. Sarah had got over her fear of being naked and had happily learnt to walk around minus them. Having a house full of teenagers certainly tested and challenged this new found sense of openness and love of it.

Feeling EarthHeart

Facebook you're a saucy little devil you, what a clever facilitator one is. Life had dropped an open invitation to experience nature as God, God as nature... a healing, in an open space named appropriately EarthHeart. A picturesque summer camp set in the beautiful Heart of the Forest of Dean, appropriately situated in the heart of the country too.

God, will this latest adventure test the husbands' patience some more? How beautiful that he had not questioned my inner desires thus far, but only offered unconditional support and blessings? But dear one, this calling is far greater than you or I? Sarah cannot stop it, like a red rag to a bull, charging forward with full on passionate force.

Red bull fingertips responding quicker than Michel Flatly on point. Boom, click, sent, done, herb tea, relax, meditate. Graciously, Sarah did allow the husband to walk in from work, take off his boots and offer him a nice cup of strong builder's tea before informing him of her next experience for self-expansion.

Sure I noted several immediate grey hairs sprout up, with a few more wrinkles etched in his brow. Dear me, what is this woman going through, flickered his sensitive eyes. Has her family trauma taken her mental health status to levels he could not reach? Could not comprehend anymore? Making her quit her professional teaching role and relinquish family mother duties?

Wouldn't you suffer too if your own mother suffered many years of manic depressive episodes? Family and friend's suicides and drug addictions? Witnessed a beloved Father's decline in health and untimely passing? To endure grief, soul family tragedy left right and centre? Soul family members struggling to help me, help each other or even help themselves? Professional health worker's hands tied with red tape protocol and prescribed medication therapy assistance only?

Sarah knows this sounds really depressing for some, comforting to others, oxymoron time lol, but as human beings we all suffer or experience the same emotions just at very different stages of one's life. It is a parallel life we all live in, same same. A question that one should ask himself or herself is this....Does one live by choice or live by chance?

What Sarah has noted (however, during her journey thus far, Sarah might change her feelings on this one further down the line, be warned, just sharing. Always one for keeping one in suspenders, er I mean in suspense like on your toes) is this...heart centred connection to others, felt at present moment influences vibrational energy, whether positive or negative. That's it.

Death is a fact of life, we all shed our physical bodies. What is key, Sarah feels, is this: it is how we live in them, respect and take care of them, express ourselves in them, honor them, honor ourselves through others in them that counts.

Sarah used to think, in her former reality, that she was a mere single vessel, wondering around the earth, interacting with others from time to time, occasionally abusing the body, punishing it for its deep yearning for something by shutting it up with alcohol or a sneaky fag, saving aimlessly for an activity led, wonderfully happy retirement. Something great to look forward to, this is what we are sedated to believe. Work your body 9-5pm relentlessly in the week, get pissed at weekends, enjoy yourself, reward oneself with a take away curry and a bottle of wine. Week in week out, month in month out. Save, save, save for a retirement you will enjoy with your beloved, that is if they make it, Dad you showed me that one! Did you get to enjoy the benefits and fruits of your labour in your physical body?

Why is it we are conditioned to save for this precious day? Hahaha fucking hahaha, what a joke. Happy retirement everyone!

Me? Sarah is a realist, no bullshit, sanguine truth seeker. She is looking for a way to live organically, ethically, with joy in the heart seeping from the pores and truth in the soul. Oh my good gracious me, Sarah, you are such a mischievous imp! What, you can't find your life plan? Is it under the sofa or in the secret drawer?

Internal GPS and gut feeling suggested that this place, EarthHeart, would reveal something more, to showcase the longing that was growing in the heart.

It was relatively easy to cancel the up and coming gym yoga classes. To be fair, corporate firms can readily replace any yoga teachers at the drop of a hat. We are so many. One particular class I felt rather reluctant to cancel though because I had really connected with a great bunch of middle aged, curvaceous, burnt out, angst, longing for their freedom of spirit, youthful and flexible selves. Sound familiar to you? Is Sarah describing her former, loveless, pre-Indian yogini former self? The once lumpy girl with a new penchant for helping/inspiring others?

Awoken by the sweet song of the birds tweeting, thanked life 3 times, jumped out of bed, pulled back the thermal curtains to reveal the most gorgeous early morning sunrise. This was a good sign. Coffee supped, car loaded, goodbyes and hugs exchanged, Sarah jumped into her trusty VW and headed off once more down the M6, M5 familiar carriageway.

Bursting to get out of this traditionally narrow minded, little northern town just outside the gloriously rainy city of Manchester. Lowry wasn't wrong when he painted those match stick men and matchstick cats and dogs. Gloriously gloomy. Lack of spontaneity, only displaying fear, culturally bound Zombies R 'US climate lol...

Tapped destination into internal Sat Nav, Forest of Dean. Got it, felt location in the bones.

Friends found it hilarious that I didn't actually posses an actual physical, electrical talking Sat Nav. Mine was much better though as it was powered by the universal life force, bar a few missed road junctions, it always remained an accurate source.

Did however, contemplate purchasing said item after a strange incident that occurred in the middle of nowhere, somewhere in between the Welsh valleys. Sarah had befriended a 1980's throwback lonely male, complete with mullet, ear hoop, handle bar moustache and donning a well loved sheep skin jacket. Bless him, I couldn't understand a word he said, nor could I get rid of the darling. Sarah only wanted directions!

Sarah really does try to keep her energy locked in, but at times finds it really hard when its just very present, which men really love to soak up. This was something Sarah had started to observe more and more. Remember the mantra, it's the 21st it's really ok to politely tell a male to fuck off.

Several hours later, albeit slightly distracted by Welsh, will not refer to as sheep shagger boyo, arrived safely to end destination... EarthHeart.

A generous hearted manager, assisted my being back and forth with the crucial wheelbarrow trips needed organize ones Hotel California. The 4-star poster bed, silky sheets, fluffy pink eye mask and such like.

At a glance, present beings oddly reminded Sarah of the characters in The Lion, the Witch and the Wardrobe. Sarah noticed that she had firmly stepped into the bubble of EarthHeart, portraying yet another character, playing yet another role in yet another movie production. How consciousness loved to go through these series of characters and dramas in order to awaken...Lol.

Sarah sensed that she was falling through a hole in the universe, while briskly assembling the lodgings with lump hammer at the ready. She was indeed a clever bunny and getting quicker now using practical skills single handedly.

Pup tent successfully up, bedroom quarters looking rather luxurious and inviting, decide on settling in for a comfy snuggle, the velvet fleece blanket demanding so. Made obligatory coffee then opened the first chapter of Abraham Hicks, Law of Attraction-lent to me by a very special soul. It read:

Hold this book in your hand, feel its energy, absorb it and when the life is ready one will open it and begin to read it and then vibrationally, a whole new paradigm will awaken within you.

Wow, how did it know all that? I had done the very same; not yet, not yet, not yet, not ready yet. Famous words.

Skimming through the pages, noted more new language. Sarah was in the middle of a forest and her friend YouTube didn't have a strong enough signal to connect at the time. Sarah had more luck connecting with badgers and hedgehogs than Wi-Fi. Needed to explore this terminology further, jotted to self in further reading notebook.

Later on, an interesting, informal introductory meeting was shared by the Queen of EarthHeart herself. A relaxed cooking rota system was announced which was to take place over an open plan outdoor fire, complete with lookalike witch's cauldron and black cast iron kettle.

Sarah placed the obligatory condiments and chamomile herb teas in the shared kitchenette. She returned a few cheat spicy sauce packets to her bat cave. Knowing full well of their inadequacy in comparison to the huge cooking pot. Insignificant bring really.

Sarah had experience of cooking for hundreds now, she understood about taste, quality and quantity. Her recent Buddhafields blessings in the kitchens contributed to that.

Not feeling the energy to offer any cooking skills just yet, Sarah opted to see it in action before successfully rising to the challenge and thus creating an edible dish. Nor had she arrived fully in the mystic valley. Instead, she enjoyed sitting around the communal camp fire, conversing little but observing everything, the quirks, mannerisms, the personalities of the souls who had arrived and attracted themselves to this universal flow. An intriguing bunch to say the least. Sarah initially couldn't feel her way through, felt complexities in its place and was all too aware of the tingling feeling in her gut. Something made her feel slightly uneasy. As if she sensed a pre-test, a mighty force, an impending challenge to her strength/weakness of character, way before the camp had even started.

One thing was for certain though, the scene was beautifully set in a reclusive valley, awash with greenery, wild flowers, honey bees, acorn trees, mist and dewy lawns, typical scenes reminiscent of a Rembrandt work of art.

From the conditioned parents, Sarah had been brought up to be well-mannered and honest, especially in a new environment and meeting strange people for the first time. Back in the day when ones' reputation was paramount, it was really important to give a good impression and all that. Respect your elders, say 'nowt or thee'll get a clowt'. Familiar with these figures of speech? I am.

The Queen of EarthHeart was a die hard advocator of God in nature, nature is God, so beautifully projected this on web too. Packed a punch it did, crisp as Mohammed Ali, peace be upon him, deeply inside.

What a remarkable woman. Celtic and Gothic in appearance. Make up free, organic, and natural. Majestically roaming around her kingdom, checking upon its running order, making sure everything ran smoothly, tickety boo. Her hair was long with swirling, dark, curls, held together in sweet pigtails using delicately placed strands of other hair, bouncing in the moist air, forming tighter ringlets around her angular jaw. Her protective 4-legged companion, apricot in contrast, permanently alert and a loyal companion, a constant at her side.

Sarah loved the quaint little caravans that served as servant's quarters, which were nestled at the bottom of the vegetable garden. Noting the juiciest, red, shiny tomatoes growing in abundance in the greenhouse there. Nearly as good as the ones Aunty Iris' grew back home, the ones she used in her Spanish salads. Now that was a real tasty treat. Weren't all your Mum's friends fondly referred to as Aunty back in day?

Admiring the picture perfect moment, Sarah sat down on a bespoke oak bench, complete with beautiful knots to lovingly finger, to shelter from the glare of the mid morning sun, appreciating the shade of a magnificent oak tree.

Sarah imagined herself here, knee deep in the snow in her Hunter Wellies and duck down jacket, casually mulching out the veggie allotment, pottering around tending softly to the wares, talking to them if need be, just as insane as Prince Charles' habit. The karma yoga experience in the holy city of Rishikesh had expressed the want for greater sensitivity in cultivating and successfully growing vegetables. A trait needed to be explored if Sarah wanted to become a successful grower.

Oh yes Sarah, you would be like a pig in shit here. I could hear Monkey Mind's suggestion loud and clear, even though he was away again on vacation for his own enlightenment. In another dimension somewhere in the hemisphere.

Hopefully, lost somewhere in Monkey Mind outer space, she thought. He had been doing her head in of late and specifically in Rishikesh, a constant loving nag, I mean presence. Sarah had started to enjoy the freedom and lighter weight on her shoulders without him. In the nicest possible way of course.

The camaraderie built increasingly over our first few days camp together, particularly so in the delightful shared preparation of meals. Sarah really loved the kitchen Tantra and banter whilst chopping, slicing, dicing and lovingly preparing the lunch and evening meals that took quite a lot of energy to do well outside. A beautiful auric unfolding.

It had been a while since Sarah had experienced this form of kitchen Tantra, other than in Buddhafields and many moons ago when the children were little. She fondly remembers baking lovely little fairy cakes with them, Mary Berry eat your heart out. But as their own fairy wings grew, so did their own taste for adventure. It was a higher probability to find them swigging alcopops on the local park with their little pixie friends, than share any such activity with the mother hen. Gestures which get lost in transit, per se. The norm.

Affectionately recollecting the times at Christmas too, when it would be typical to have a customary pie bake off with the hubby. Seldom shared precious cookery moments together. Friends would be faced with the challenge of selecting their preferred winning dish. Would they opt for the taste of my meat combo feast over his impressive poultry based, sweetcorn and mushroom roux sauce puff pastry topped eloquent lattice work d'art? Guess who always won?

Ego minds to be congratulated for a sincere, light hearted laugh at our expenses.

That's the true nature of food, another expression of love. Humans forget this. Merely brainwashed into thinking that there is no time in the day to cook, nourish, nurture and care for one another. Make time. Make love.

Why feed your cells toxic convenience foods? Over sugared, over salted and over E numbered, over everything. You wouldn't put diesel in an unleaded car would you? Such un-love.

A very dear friend of mine, who won't mind me sharing this, has recently been given the all clear and dismissal from hospital after a very serious life threatening condition. What did he do, immediately after his encouraging diagnosis? Return to the pub for his usual tipple and consummation of his weekly 7 ping, ping meals. Ping, ping, lifeless, ping ping off, keep your poisonous chemicals that I wouldn't feed a dog as they rot organs from inside out. Not to mention diminish the body soul mind combo.

A hearty colourful soup was in progress for supper: the purples from the beetroot, oranges from the suede's, neutral tones from the chick peas and the clean contrast of the cauliflower florets. It all looked so very tantalizing to the eyes while being lovingly stirred around in the big, open pot with a big, wooden heavy laden to match. How on earth one managed to cook so well and in such large amounts over an open fire, eluded Sarah. Although balance, fire mitt and technical skill comes to mind.

Tentatively, Sarah offered to help contribute with the washing up after dinner. This would help to break the ice on a smaller, more intimate scale.

Sarah felt a tad lost in the growing army of EarthHeart summer camp campers, swelling in number as the weekend progressed. Many had arrived/landed on various occasions and were not in the least backwards in coming forwards in meaning.

Increasingly, the camp fire soothed any uneasiness and developed more meaningful trust. It takes an awful lot of energy to establish and maintain a hearty, warming fire.

Munch, munch, crunch, crunch...munch...crunch... Sarah awoke rather bemused and disorientated to an unfamiliar sound coming from the porch area? Had something gotten in in the night?

Peeped through the zipper, expecting a giant, ferocious badger or the like, to spot a really cute tiny hedgehog, that had slipped in under the ground sheet, helping itself to a secret banana stash and a few nibbles out of a secret apple stash too. Karma for not sharing and putting in communal kitchen area, Sarah recorded! Drat! One can never escape Karma!

Bless its cotton socks she thought with a content smirk, zipped up the zipper and rolled over back into the warm spot of the fleecy blanket for an additional snooze. No dreams recollected. The Indian Highlights tour had certainly eradicated that dreary episode and chapter of one's life. Though a necessary, healing important contributory aspect of Sarah's transformation. Thanks to life.

Awoke several hours later, observed the dark green shade on the tent becoming lighter due to the morning rays of the sun. Crawled out of the warm pit, threw on some comfy yogi leggings and made way, empty stomach and all to the communal, multi purpose bell tent for a dynamic, hardcore ashtanga get me up, get me going dynamic, type of session.

"Feel free if you want to come join me this morning," Sarah enthused to the awakening neighbours, rolling the yoga mat under the arm. Just adored the internal setting for the practice, strewn with antler horns, candles, twizzle sticks and comfy bean chairs, carefully arranged on the sacred EarthHeart alter under a fluffy sheep skin rug. However, a few gentle beings withered under Sarah's over enthusiastic, body alignment assistance and soon abandoned practice and left.

Come on Sarah, were is your compassion, you have been told about this before? I thought you had a handle on this? Came a voice from somewhere. Was it the shadow self talking this time? Wasn't Monkey Mind because he wasn't here? Must be?

From the opening gap in the bell tent, whilst still in headstand, Sarah could make out swirling smoke, bellowing down into the Mother Earths crust. She could clearly grasp animated onesies' inclusive of bunny ears bobbing about, bouncing around in the atmosphere, magnetized by a big, black steamy pot of 'double, double, toil and trouble, fire burn and cauldron bubble.' She too could smell, the enticing unpretentious aroma of the simmering oatmeal. She felt hungry also.

A little chalkboard plaque outside the community bell tent detailed the morning's schedule, which included an initial morning Meeting of Hearts.

The experience was a bit like a carpet session for primary school kids that Sarah had formerly, lovingly held. Although on this occasion, it was directed for adults with inner child conflict blockages and more, she sensed.

One by one, campers were passed a sacred twizzle stick and if one felt the need to share from the heart, whilst holding the said item, one could. Without fear or discernment. This was simply an opportunity, to be seen, be heard and be held.

Upon receipt of this consecrated wooden object, Sarah did not feel the urge to share much, just gratitude for arriving safely. Appreciating at the time how very uncomfortable and daunting this experience can feel to children.

Make a deep fat note to self here Sarah, next time you teach or recreate this platform for sharing, remember how intrusive one can feel. How others can potentially feel if their story holds such vulnerabilities that are painful to share.

A strong divine feminine energy rippled through the circle of trust, escalating in heat between a few female members. One could not blame them for their solidarity or firmly established sisterhood comradeship. Akin to those relationships formed in high school. The giggling girly, fierce and popular type that you so want to be in but you can't because you belong to the gingered haired, glasses wearing geek gang, whose parents are professional banker types.

Rounds of applause erupted around the circle when a very sensual female Shakti shared a very pleasing remark, something along the lines of being recently 'treated like a princess and boned to the moon' by an extremely beautiful conscious male.

Well, didn't Sarah just love that statement. She was loving every minute of this juicy circle of trust. Now bearing in mind Sarah's recent Buddhafields antics. She was not a wilting flower type, but oh my goodness, jaw dropping material which fed the heart space further, emotional soul fuel.

Sorry but not sorry for not letting you in on that very juicy, enlightening knowledge. It is not a Terry's Chocolate Orange. But Sarah couldn't resist sharing that little jewel with you.

Furthermore, Sarah will not share any further intimate details with you. A circle of trust should never be broken.

Suffice to say, use one's imagination or draw from your own reality and one won't be too far off the truth. Deep within the heart space one is longing for the same same thing.

Human beings...we all suffer similar, to bring one closer to one's truth. Often stories include many shocking experiences. But once you can tell your own story without crying, you know that you have been healed.

Down in the forest, The Queen of EarthHeart summoned her troops to a mid-morning silent gathering. In groups of the sacred number 3, campers were asked to go on a silent walking meditation and retrieve a noun that filled the heart with gratitude.

Hhmmm. Sarah liked this idea a lot, she loved planning little interesting, thought provoking kinks for children. This was a clever adult version though.

Her triad partnership included a silky, dark, long haired South Korean Goddess wearing a turquoise night slip and a shy sensitive English Rose dressed in pinky floral. Did Sarah project a loud mouthed northern lass in grubby, tomboyish swag? Probably...lol.

Off we tiptoed into the woods, mindfully stepping over the bracken so as not to damage the souls of the feet. Aware of the juicy mud as it squelched between the toes. Walking, in silence, ducking under branches, weaving through the trees, carefully not allowing it to flick back and take another's eye out, until we came to a clearing in the distance which just opened up and swallowed us in whole.

Amazingly, we had collectively stumbled across a Raphaelite painting, complete with vibrant yellow water lilies, neon algae which cast a luminous glow over the murky, clay based water. Noticing the sunlight pouring through the evergreen trees casting a magnificent reflection over the pond. Plus, hearing the sound of harmonious humming birds singing high in the trees. In unison, we sat down on the banks of the millpond, synchronistically giving one another space for contemplation and self enquiry.

Sarah closed her eyes and began to meditate, feeling the silence, beauty and stillness present. What did this vision suggest to Sarah? After a few moments, she opened her eyes and gazed, Drishna style, softening the gaze ever so slightly resting the eye lids closer together at a distant spot.

115

What struck her the most was the reflection mirrored immaculately back from the murky topped surface of the pond water, reflecting perfectly mirror images of greens, golden yellows hues and orange tones with such ease.

Sarah immediately drew from this snapshot moment that in life human beings offer the very same service to humanity.

How can I be of service for you today? Please be a good mirror so one can see oneself clearly.

Concluding that there are many mirrors in life, reflecting both essential positive and negative aspects of our being, both are equally as important for growth. To reflect our being, our personalities and our internal God self if we seek this. Only what is God's intention? Keep on looking in these reflecting mirrors until one cannot see oneself? One's dramas? One's story up until the point of purification and the truth?

Thoughts of such intensity were running like wild fire through the mind. Will check in with Monkey Mind later if one is granted Wifi connectivity. Pretty hit and miss due to the dense, inverted location. Put that thought on the back burner for later, Sarah darling.

Carefully retracing our steps back to camp after wistfully deepening our connection with nature, Sarah realized that she was empty handed and had not collected a trophy noun to return to camp with. After several moments, she mischievously spied some rabbit poo droppings in the foliage, reached down and grabbed a handful and placed them gently in her jean pocket. The other fairies had a white feather and a pine cone between them.

The meeting point was strategically centred in-between a male and female acorn tree, exactly 5 metres apart. Earlier, Sarah had hugged both of them out of curiosity. Upon examination, the female felt much softer to hold in contrast to the hardness of the male. Surprised?

How anyone could ever release anger towards one, one could not ever know. Sarah had heard several cries of 'Fuck Off,' plus other obscurities from lovely Shakti's mouths, who had wandered off into the woods to release a bit of pent up moon cycle energy. Moon cycles eh?

Sarah had yet not had the experience. Nor did she really have the desire, as generally speaking, she did not carry the emotion of anger in her body. Loss, yes, fear yes. However, she was working on those.

Additionally, to her, trees were a symbolic, phallic icon of consciousness, maintaining a secret underground sophisticated, vibrational life support network system, commuting valuable nutrients and dispersing life force energy to those trees that need it most to survive. As humans we cannot see this infrastructure with the naked eye. Yet this support system is in place. Isn't life magical?

In relation to beings, one is similar to this underground support system. As we are both so much more than our trunks, that one can see with the naked eye.

Yoga you beautiful vibrational essence you. Thank you so much for helping one feel the body, for getting right into it and helping see the simplicity in natural ways of living. For the habitual one takes a lot of effort, over effort. The beauty of yoga is really a way to minimize and conserve energy for better purposes.

Definitely not a way to leave the body like some like to practice.

The rabbit poo received a huge eruption of belly laughs. Naughty, mischievous Sarah. More so, from the few children campers. The silent walking meditation now officially declared over.

A vast array of beautiful, natural resources which were collected from the ground, that were beautifully presented in an artistically shaped arc.

Sarah un-folded the methodology behind her pickings.

Well, she began, woodland creatures don't need permission to off load their shit on Mother Earth for she is abundant. Likewise, for beings, why hold onto one's shit, let it go, Mother Earth supports you fully if you allow it.

Others proceeded to identify more sensitive aspects of humanness; the symbolism of a delicate feather, sensitive and gentle in a world lost to ego mind numbing grasping, cold hearts and materialism.

How refreshing, being reminded of God's voice through the vehicle of nature. Sadly, us humans have forgotten to tap into this ability, conditioned by constant Monkey Mind speak.

It's so important to switch of that brainwashing TV and reconnect with nature as often as possible. Get outdoors and feel the seasons. Explore, feel, connect.

After a long day musing, Sarah's male energy needing absorbing so she decided to sit under the female Shakti oak tree, to mellow out a bit. She sat in lotus position, back up tight next to the bark, crossed her legs, closed her eyes and began to meditate.

After a few brief moments, she could sense an additional presence nearby, in fact only 5 metres away and sat mirroring her exact demeanor, under the early evening shade of the male Shiva, powerhouse oak tree.

Momentarily, she opened her eyes.

The one and only Monkey Mind had dropped in for a surprise visit. Like a pre-dental check up.

Although, he didn't say anything, his presence alone was felt enough, as he sat quietly, eyes closed, leaning against the bark of the Shiva oak tree.

Only the pretty rainbow arc signified distance between the pair of us, rabbit poo and all. Blinked twice, yes, it was really him, blinked again and he was gone.

Sarah felt like a warm, toasted pink marshmallow inside, ready to devour. She felt so deliciously palpable.

The Queen triumphantly blew the concha shell; it's whistling vibrational call summoning the cooks for evening duties. Sarah's cue to return to base and get scrubbed up. Tonight, it was her turn.

What to prepare for the troops? The nymph co-workers proposed several options, in the end we plumped for a green and brown dish. In tune with the colours of the natural environment around us. We lovingly piled green beans, spinach, broccoli, sprouts, mushrooms, peppers, brown rice and quinoa on top of one another in the smoking hot, cauldron, carefully mixing the prana, the life, with fire mitt in one hand, heavy ladle in another. Sarah's naughty personality suggested sneaking back to the pup tent to collect a sneaky pre-prepared curry sauce packet for added taste. However, additional lashings of salt and pepper seemed to do the trick just nicely and thankful hand gestures over the food to thank life for providing such abundance, gave plenty of added taste.

Early dusk, and hungry guts and mouths are sat patiently around the camp fire, eagerly waiting to devour the delicious nutrition bubbling away, simmering nicely in the open air and under un polluted star filled sky.

Did our camp enjoy and feel the abundant love poured into our food? Certainly, appreciation came in many onomatopoeic forms, in various tones of ooos and arrhhrrs.

Sarah and the sous chefs hugged and winked collectively, sending the oxytocin levels through the roof. Bliss, all has been fed well in the EarthHeart summer camp that evening.

The evening was filled with more heart opening camp fire stories and evening song. And silence, of perfectly just sitting observing the dancing, amber flames.

The lullaby of the gentle guitar strings and shared poetry couldn't be bought for a top ticket at a West End Show.

Sarah started feeling the warmth of the contents of the belly expanding up into the heart centre, travelling up into the head space, sending sleepy, cosy signals to the body.

A beautiful, appreciative shoulder rub levitated Sarah to her crib. Sarah sang her goodnights and then departed from this peaceful and tranquil energy, from bodies lying perfectly still but harmoniously on the ground, absorbing the heat from the slowly, fizzling out embers.

Sarah gave her teeth a quick rinse and placed her comfy Ali baba sweat pants on, snuggly wriggled into her mummy bag, then flicked on her solar powered energy glow lamp to read through a few pages of Abraham.

Mmmm, so Sarah feels like she belongs in the manifest category, definitely does not feel like a projector or generator. Very interesting these Human Design principles, just another term, figure of speech for yet another example of a mask one could wear right now in the beautiful life!

Task is, to figure out which one one has been served with, that is if you feel a calling to do so? Or simply put, what is God's plan for you? What is your truth, your soul purpose? Your God consciousness? What to find out?

Sarah was trying to figure hers out, at all costs too.

The beloved family had every right to think that I was going crazy. I most certainly looked like I was. For up to now, I had seemed like I had no direction, no purpose, no structure, no fathomable explanation to this journey or culmination of experiences to date. Absolutely nothing to feedback to the family and friends that all was really fine and dandy. That life remained sweet.

Definitely, sending off signals of wasting money and what for? Sickness and depression? Had I been brainwashed? How could I abandon the blessed feminine daughter? The very beautiful, Shakti that I was blessed to borne? Elf like in appearance with very beautiful almond shaped eyes of blue steel and a cute, upturned button nose.

Yes, Sarah wanted to remain perfectly present with her beloved daughter, she alone was the ultimate test, the biggie test of attachment. Supporting evidence to the life that Sarah was for sure, in service to that which is far greater than the body. Sarah's absolute test of devotion to the truth.

Sarah knows and feels this, each being has their own journey home to the truth. Perfectly so as God had intended. Sarah cannot interfere with this, nor dictate so.

Each being is wonderfully born alone, bred alone until the body dies alone, yet beautiful beings, one is never alone. God, consciousness, awareness, divine intelligence, whatever, is always omnipresent.

The early morning rainfall has scampered the morning camp planned activities. The Queen proposes a cathartic dance healing in the Temple to rejoicing cheers from the crowds. The observer, observing being observed by Sarah, felt a little wince inside, like a little whimpering puppy in a corner, alone abandoned and unwanted in the puppy pound. She drew reference from the Buddhafields festival dance healing experience.

Sarah thought for a while, perhaps in a smaller, more intimate circle of trust, she would be able to surrender the body and let go a little more? She had established a really nice connection with a little French family with 3 adorable siblings, in perfect descending height order.

As the dance beats kicked in, Sarah gravitated to the innocence of their natural innate, un-spoilt pure state, gently holding their hands and swaying in time to the mellow, slow flowing, Root chakra, Mooladhara activational tunes, feeling the easiness, slowly, gently allowing the hips to wake up and surrender to the dance. Ok this felt comfortable.

The tempo uplifted, to a more frenzied, hedonistic, tribal drum beat vibe so energize and open up the sacred sacral, the Swadhisthana, the all encompassing Mother Earth, mother of fruits, life creator and destroyer.

Momentarily lost in a hypnogogic trance, the eyes glanced across the oak paneled polished wooden floor, to observe Asian beauty, dancing carefree on the lawn like a very graceful butterfly, turquoise slip less and so enjoying the rain droplets splash over her naked visible body. Her wide, cream panties covered her modesty bits but due to the rainfall and transparency of the material, one could see her dark pubic mound in all its glory.

The tempo picked up even further, woooah, males moaning and hollering deeply, in contrast to females shrieking wildly, sending out various emotional vibrations.

Bodies uncontrollably falling to the knees and rolling around on the floor, not in gentle honor and respect for the body, but to get rid of abhorrence.

The resulting children's cries firstly sent Sarah's ears, then heart, then stomach into a deep paralysis. What to do? She offered to take the children drawing and reading with nice books, stickers, teddy bears and warm, fleecy blankets and snuggles. Sarah flipped into supportive teacher mode. This she liked, a lot more.

Mummy's screams and obscenities could be heard echoing around the woodland, prompting natural childlike questioning. What does Sarah do? Reply with age appropriate answers, to sooth a tender enquiring mind, and draw a colourful family home complete with rosy apple tree, chimney smoke, pastel curtains and flowers.

Mummy and Daddy returned from their purification on very different agendas. Sarah left their tent, this was not her karmic commitment.

Time for a rest and a feed before an afternoon spent pond dipping.

The Queen of EarthHeart certainly resonated deeply on a profound level with the summer camping campers. No wonder, after many years' experience of psychiatric psychotherapy. This Queen bee knew solutions and responded very beautifully and naturally as they arose/cropped up. This Queen was a warrior fighter and could hold space extremely well, especially under dark womb energy that spilled out during some intimate sharings.

Ultimately, this made Sarah feel rather uncomfortable. It stood the hairs on her neck right up. Sarah's teaching practice and professional development stood no familiar ground in these neck of the woods. One needed a certificate from the university of life. Not a Bachelor of Science University Degree.

Something had come up. Did Sarah need or want this type of platform in nature to satisfy her own deep down fears and blockages, that had accumulated over the years from the events in her own story?

An afternoon, leisurely stroll to a hidden pond, buried deep in the woodland scrub, filled with light chit chat and other pleasantry exchanges, was to unfolded on our next EarthHeart summer camp to do list.

A beautiful pile of colourful different textured pants, tops and socks addressed the clay banks. As each layer was peeled off, a discerning lone fisherman checked his cigarette several times after each inhalation.

Sarah screamed as her naked body slipped down the sticky embankment. She tried to grab hold of the tall reeds directly popping out from under the water as if to steady her from falling into the cold, but fresh water too quickly. Too late, she plopped in and let out a huge, high pitched scream, as the sticky clay squelched between her toes and the cold current gripped her body with an intense electrifying shock that ran up the spine.... Shakti Kundalini! Queen bee roared from her observant perch at the side of river bank. "Hahahah, that's what resonates with Sarah, the water element," she squealed in delight. She had guessed my Achilles heal.

A lovely fellow soul in the huge, strapping body of Tom, lent out a guiding hand and with a gentle swoop, lifted me up into his arms so that Sarah could fit her tiny body, pale in comparison, around his large waist and support herself by placing her tiny arms around his thick, strong neck. The water was a little too deep for her to stand up in alone.

Observers observed a real life work of art painting in progress, containing 2 supporting naked bodies, bobbing up and down and weaving through the golden yellow lily pads and glistening algae. Sarah stared deeply into Tom's sensitive soul and sensed his yearning for intimacy, for deep soul connection.

Sarah could sense love vibrating in his lingam. Sarah stayed wonderfully present and held this moment with love in her heart only.

The former self would have felt that she had been sexually violated. However, this transformational self only felt compassion. The look from eyes spoke volumes. Love and trust comes from a deeper connection served over a lengthy time period. Tom's adored former wife sadly passed from cancer several years earlier and how he worshipped the very ground she walked on, raising their young boys single handedly, with such devotion, one could weep in loving admiration. One could feel that deeply transmitted through all of his very beautiful fibers.

Sarah released the grip, slid from his grasp like a slippery eel, jumped up the muddy embankment as quickly as possible, and threw her clothes on to keep from catching a chill. Bless that man.

Snow white and the seven dwarves had made their hasty departure back to base camp, several moments earlier. Sarah hurriedly tried to catch them up, dodging the bracken, nettles and wiry prickles underfoot. Following the decibel cries of 'Fuck you' through a zig zag of trees. Sarah approached a tree, knelt down and opened the mouth but the only word to fall out was "Thank you."

Sarah is a student of love, that's it.

Sarah collapsed in a heap in her sacred pup pup tent, for a much needed cutch with herself. Flipped open Abraham for some much needed inspiration and some encouraging words to be found within the text. Some little universal code. Help me please?

Later in the evening after a very moving heart circle sharing, a random great, big, whopping puppy pile sprung up. One that Sarah had not experienced before, and so stayed on the outskirts out of comfort zone options. Somehow Tom had managed to wiggle over and place his giant paws around my tiny waist. Sarah was very overcome with emotion and found it difficult to connect on that level of intimacy. She did enjoy the heart connectivity but not the feelings of intensity and longing, maybe Sarah's radar was far too emphatic?

Sarah withdrew from the senses, Pratyahara was on the cards, she heard her Guru's mantra in her head, 8 rounds of sun salutations in the dimming glow of the sunset. That she did too. Bliss.

An evening stroll through some woodland, to buy some chocolate at a nearby service station, felt like an escape job from Alcatraz. A beautiful spotting of a family of deer which scurried off sharpish into the distance on noticing my presence, left me alone with mind that is churning curd tenfold. The self wants chocolate, must get to garage, must have chocolate. Sarah hastily sidesteps great pools of mud, in eager anticipation of receiving a quicker oral fix.

Once inside the garage, a sharp dawning occurred for Sarah, the garage attendant, the self service customers, the petrol attendant, were all from the dimension that Sarah used to live in. Sarah immediately felt a sharp pull towards this paradigm and wanted to return, to leave the EarthHeart Bubble Syndrome in all of its raw, beautiful glory.

Sarah decided to leave the camp, there and then. A calling came from inside. Early to bed, early to rise, early to leave and to hit the road and escape this malady. Space was needed to internalize the steep learning curve.

Treated like a princess and boned to the moon, came to help deconstruct the 4-star luxury camping pad. We took the thing down quicker that Usain Bolts 10 seconds 100 metre sprint. Wow, Sarah was getting really quick at whipping this bugger up and down in record time. Maybe one should go in the Guinness book of records for this technical, practical mean feat.

Had to laugh at the very Bedouin nature that Sarah had created for herself. How perfectly simple camping outdoors in nature was. Very harmonious. No massive heating bills, no cleaning chores, no menial house duties to constantly juggle. The worst of it avoiding Sarah's full on pet hate.... toilet cleaning. How very idealist having a toilet compost system instead.

One evening during an obligatory camp fire; a tale emerged about a wild boar, foraging amongst the sewage pit, down in the basement of the good 'ole compost toilets.

If that had happened to her, goodness knows how Sarah would have felt; knickers dropped, legs spread wide eagled across the wooden toilet seat, peering down to witness such a spectacle during a morning bowel movement. Funnily scary.

Rocked up the beloved car, filling it with all Sarah's beautiful survival possessions. Feeling rather surreal as the coffee press, muddy boots and foam futon mattress were thrown in. Sarah has always been rather an organized disorganized being. However, left just enough room to check out other vehicles and traffic.

Bearing in mind, the last few day's experiences were rather heavyweight to say the least, nearly as funky fresh as the 7-foot Queen of the blue elves saga in Buddhafields. Things were about to take an even further twist, step up a notch, kick up a gear, EarthHeart you little minx, you never cease to surprise me. My EarthHeart sank as one reversed out the drive to an awaiting plethora of beings, strategically centralized on the farm gate, as if coal strike protestors. Oh no what to do?

Sarah envisaged a lengthy bon voyage scene to exit, before glancing down at her rose quartz bracelet, bought for her as a gift from a very dear friend... 'Surround yourself with the colour purple, my darling, this is the highest colour which will protect you.'

"Why are you leaving so soon? Your energy is so healing, please stay longer!" Begged one.

Sarah knew what to do. She took off her rose quartz bracelet, "Here lovely, I will miss you too, take this as a gift, as a reminder of right now to stay very present at each moment and love yourself first. Then love will flow most naturally to others."

Wow, Sarah didn't know were those words came from.

Adding, "Don't worry if you lose it even, the sentiment and the moment has been signed, sealed and delivered."

Hugs were exchanged. Rite of passage granted, smiles followed a happy Sarah down the lane.

Sarah felt too, as she hit the approaching hard shoulder, that she had learnt an awful lot of stuff and like a honey bee in pursuit of sweet nectar, had jumped from one beautiful experience to another, from one sweet fragrance to the next.

In fact, Sarah had learnt a copious amount of stuff recently, and not from textbooks solely, but from real direct experience, from real heart centred conversations, from surrender and sacrifice.

In fact, the body walking around identified in the form of Sarah felt rather pious in nature. Most honest, healthy and happy that one had felt in a while. Apart from special moments hanging out with the family, but hey ho, they thought the mother was a nutter, a meditating yogi freak, ranting on about Goddess Tara, Kali or her favourite Parvati. Her cherished Goddess' of love and transformation and power! And Thankyou too, Ganesha for removing the apparent obstacles. Such beautiful tools of the trade to equip one for such transformational purposes.

Little did they know of my nightly candle lit meditations, in search of a deeper level of truth, of the who am I kind? Nor would they know that I had always felt this way, stronger at times than others of course. Always in Gratitude for one's life anyhow.

Doris, bless her cotton socks, insisted that 'my' grounding would come from childbirth and marriage. Sarah knew differently.

Since the Spanish retreat, Sarah hadn't touched a drop of alcohol. Since the Indian Highlights tour, she resolved never to touch alcohol again. Life was far fresher through sober eyes. The body enjoyed a new found physical strengthened stability and flexibility. The major organs pumped, pulsated and internally felt joyful, with renewed vigor after 20 treadmill unhealthy years.

Sarah's cells were dancing. They were alive. Never loved as much placing sacred food into the mouth before. Thanking God profusely for daily nourishment which could feed the whole world. Thanking God daily for the joy in life to breathe each sacred breath.

Stark contrast to those whose realization offers a different outcome. For those who cannot breathe independently, riddled or blessed with some crippling disease or other.

Each and every day, Sarah thanked life for her clear, oxygenated pranayama, for the ability to deeper, cleanse the breath and for the Yoga principles learned by Jalandhara Bandha, Uddiyana Bandha and Mula Bandha combined to pack a punch in the Great Lock, the mother of locks, or the King of Breath work in yogic terms.

No way would dirty toxins again make their way anywhere near Sarah's precious mouth, or leak their way through her skin ever again. Why own a leaky bucket and leak energy when you can work on yourself and have a fool proof leak free one? Carry on walking the bridge to cross to grace my darling, if one wanders off a little to the embankment of complaining, remember gratitude and you'll head straight back over to the side of grace.

Yes, Sarah was very aware indeed of her growth, she knew as she indicated in and out of the motorways fast lanes, that her perception, intuition, deeper knowing, touch and heart space had been thrown open wide into a whole new level of being. How could one convey these deeper feelings to one's family freely, with ease and comfort, to express a more natural state of being?

The husband had always insisted that I had thought too deeply about things over the years. How could I tell him of my shift in level of perceptions? That once which was at the top of my list, materialism, was now at the bottom.

Sarah flicked the radio on, Whitney Houston's Greatest Love of all… Is inside of you, is playing, how very true. Life always speaks in magical ways. Enjoyed a right good sing song we did.

Sarah felt as though she was moving but not moving, talking but not talking, changing but not changing, you get the drift?

It is not quantum physics, its not quantifiable, it cannot be described. How does one describe expansion, consciousness expansion?

It is relativity simple to describe the stages of child development as a series of progressive steps, with preconceived benchmarks.

Spirituality? For adults?

Why yes WHSmith holds a vast section of self help spiritual books and mid life crisis books designed for predominantly women who are lost in cyber space. Where to start? What to choose? What to know?

Sarah started to feel drowsy, head was filling up with mind fog and a back log of traffic had extended the journey by 2 hours already. Therefore, an obligatory quick pit stop was needed to fill up on caffeine and relieve the bladder.

A huge queue at the services toilets spilled out across the forecourt. Sarah was not waiting around knee deep in Shakti energy just to wet the whistle.

Quick as a flash, assessing the situation, with military precision and with EarthHeart sentiments deeply embedded in the psyche already. Sarah scanned a privet bush. Jackpot, unsolicited boundaries, obscured by 2 beings scoffing saturated fats, passers by unable to notice a little me body, long skirt covering modesty, relieving bodily fluids with a smug grin on the boatrace.

Satisfied and relieved, she got behind the wheel, and drove off mindfully until a few hypnotizing hours later, Sarah was sat at a familiar junction known to her then she sharply indicated to pull over. Monkey Mind was on the blower. The synchronicity of it.

"How you doing love?" What's thee upto?" Enquired my beautiful friend.

Sarah couldn't speak, she felt numb, like she was going to explode. She didn't have a clue to to do. Could she go home? Could she inform the husband of her intimate naked swim with a very beautiful being, in the name of healing? Could she discuss the intimate details whilst prepping the obligatory Sunday roast family dinner?

Could she share how much freedom she enjoyed from her new found status? Her love of her naked form and the form of others? Was Sarah going totally mad?

Sarah dropped by a local Drivethru restaurant to connect to the free Wi-Fi, take herb tea, to contemplate and to drop an email to a beloved friend of hers in the States. A very articulate, juicy, powerful Shakti Goddess who incidentally synchronistically, had a free home available to rent in the North West.

Sarah loves the sheer beauty of high speed internet and its capacity for uber quick responses. Within the hour, Sarah arranged to pick up her house keys from a next door neighbour. My beloved friend's home was empty for a few months whilst she explored co-creation and self expansion. Beautiful.

Thankyou life, Sarah had a safe place to reflect, to feel safe, to be alone with self. To embrace fully what had been discovered through all her exploring so far.

Life you are very, very wonderful and majestic indeed.

Living Alone with the Higher Self

Turning the keys in the lock-promising tranquility. Sarah gently opened the oak wooden door to reveal a bright, clean smell and freshly painted white, uncluttered walls. In the lounge, several boxes of children's nouns were stacked up, ready for overseas shipment or a charity shop giveaway. Sarah didn't quite know other than there was a lot of baby dolls and nursery equipment staring right back at her.

Yes, the house was very minimalist but Sarah loved that. She knew the lack of clutter here would be perfect as the self could be felt more naturally too. No distractions or huge amounts of electromagnetic disturbances present either. Just a nearby peaceful Maharashi dome, which vibrationally permeated through all sinews on arrival. Sarah felt it. As did the beautiful rubber plant, which stood proudly on the window sill, soaking up the sunshine and basking in silent glory.

A beautiful next door neighbour informed Sarah not to be disturbed between the hours of 6am and 8am and 5pm until 7:30pm. Wonderful, collective meditation vibes. Sarah would feel those also. So would Monkey Mind. He would like it here too.
Next, a relatively cold shower because Sarah didn't know how to turn on the central heating system or water boiler at this point. Nor did she know how long she would be staying for, or what bills to expect. None of these logistical things had been discussed with her dearly beloved Patzy yet. It was a case of love and trust. You need a safe place to crash. So be it my darling. That was big hearted, juicy Goddess Patzy all over.
Sensing her incredible Shakti energy, Sarah slipped on her fluffy, red robe from a hook behind the bathroom door. Then placed her fluffy white bed socks on, lit some incense and candles and jumped under the bedcovers. She was feeling mentally exhausted after the unfolding day's events and needed some much deserved slumber.
On the bedside table, Sarah had casually placed her lent copy of Abraham Hicks, still unfinished, because it was a hard one to digest fully and assimilate. Sarah liked to process in bitesize chunks.

Anyhow, picked the copy up, flicked open the next chapter, held in place by a very impressive colourful rocket bookmark and began to absorb the words.

Most interestingly, Abraham started to talk about how she started channeling her higher self through meditation practice with her beloved partner. How source would use her nose to draw out letters her partner scribe down on paper whilst sitting opposite her. Then transcribe. Wow. Sarah was very intrigued. Messages from the divine. Is this true? Is it possible?

After several pages, Sarah drifted off into a deep comatose, propped up on the haunches, snuggled up in the fluffy, red robe, with the quilt covers gently resting under the chin and the Abraham book resting on the chest with the arms dangling out loosely at the sides.

At 1:03am sharply, a harsh tug from within causes Sarah to suddenly wake up with a jerky pull forwards, stir wildly at the blank walls in front and feeling panic. Internally, vomit seems to be wanting to make its way up through the esophagus.

This was another new experience. Sarah had had no dreams nor midnight disturbances since India. In fact, had slept really well and deeply for many months now. Why now?

Sarah felt the instant need to meditate. So she sat up in the bed, propped the pillows up and rolled her shoulder back and down, softly closed the eye lids and quieted the mind to return to that clear blue space. She softened the shoulders, softened the head space, drew a breath then visualized the energy filling up the heart space, the continued beautiful energy down into the mother womb, filling that space with loving presence.

When all of a sudden Sarah felt a strange uncontrollable jerk of the head, even though deep in meditation, she felt her head twisting in a circular motion round and round, gaining momentum uncontrollably. Could Sarah stop it? No. She was just the observer. OM, OO, OM, OM, these letters were circled with the entire head.

Could this be the channeling of the higher self Sarah had only just read about in Abraham? Surely not? Sarah had only just read that a few hours earlier. Had this information been internalized, projected or manifested, or all 3, so soon?

Sarah was at this moment more than happy to do absolutely nothing, no-thing about it, just be the observer and let it pass and accept.

Tears started welling up in the eyes, rolling down the cheeks before moving into fully blown sobs. Oh dear, what to do?

Sarah reached under the bed to grasp for her Ipad. Checked her Omega watch, thank you Dad, observed the USA/UK time difference, a real time connection was do-able. Skype call Patzy. That's what life suggested. She would find the exact words to comfort Sarah. So Sarah did.

Patzy was enjoying cocktails in an American local bar with her bonding partner. Full of beautiful, glowing presence and abundant joy. Sarah in the Ipad viewer looked as though she had been pulled through a hedge backwards, with her curly wig, stuck up on end, like she had just experienced an electric shock.

Sarah confided in Patzy what had just materialized in her bedroom, in her very house, with that very book that she had very lent me. Powerful stuff. Patzy was overjoyed. Told Sarah to relax, ease oneself into the process and enjoy.

Sarah tried to go back to sleep. But felt as though she was in shock or having a really wild reality submersion or dreaming the whole lot. She didn't know or really wanted to identify with anything.

However, she did eventually drop off to sleep well that evening. In the morning, she awoke to the soft morning song of the birds, chirping merrily out side. After a really good deep stretch of the arms and legs in the gorgeous presence of stillness and silence, Sarah floated downstairs to put on the usual mornings coffee press to invigorate and stimulate the senses into action.

What struck Sarah was the simplicity and grace that filed the entire space. Sarah could feel this strongly. Very unlike the haphazard, dramatic energy that she could intensely feel contained within her own family home. No matter how many times this was blessed with sage or smudge wood or filled with beautiful mantra and loving intentions. Sarah felt pulled out of alignment with source there. Although suffering is grace and not suffering at all but expansion and marvelous opportunities for growth, Sarah could not take others grasping ego any more. She had enough to deal with her own aka the grasping Monkey Mind. She so needed this tranquil space to contemplate, to go inside the internal cosmic cave of love, the eternal heart space.

Was Sarah even in control of what was happening to her? Or was she allowing it to unfold with such ferocity, that she didn't care? That she didn't understand herself fully enough yet? Sarah knew only this…that she knew nothing…no-thing. From then on she quit reading any further books too.

The mornings ritualistic black coffee was enjoyed immensely, hugged in a fluffy, red robe, sat at the dining room table, staring outside at a very beautiful hypnotic, masculine father figure willow tree, trying to reach its branches through the patio doors as if to share a loving embrace.

Several playful birds caught one's attention, and reminded Sarah of the times visiting the lovely Doris in the mental hospital, and when she would lovingly talk to them and feed them her saved crumbs from mealtimes. The birds were her friends; they were Sarah's too.

Sarah threw a handful of sunflower seeds out onto the patio table that proudly stood in the middle of the garden, good shot, many landed in the middle. The cheeky Magpies gained monopoly.

Sarah returned to the dining table some more, closed her eyes gently to feel very present, then witnessed another strange experience. Before going into that deeper, meditative state, she sensed her head had started to roll again, circling the Om sign and holy sideways figure of 8. Under this tranquil state, Sarah felt her fingers hover over the keyboard of the Ipad and begin to start sensitively typing. She didn't know what she was typing but knew that something was spelling out something, that words were formed under her fingers that she could only sensualize.

Sarah asked the question internally. What it is that you want me to do?

Was this the 'higher self' conversing with one again this morning?

Sarah had already experienced being lifted out her body, per se, during yoga practice so was not at all attached or freaked out by the kundalini experience at all. Sarah had actually experienced being thrown to the floor before now. Playing African drum beats, foot massage or shoeless outdoor jogs in nature, usually did the grounding trick.

Remembering the time once, when Sarah sat there forming the shape of the holy cross, over and over again with her head, and subsequently, had to sit outside in nature, cuddled in a grounding blanket, barefoot; only to observe Monkey Mind, staring down at her from the bedroom window, with a concerned, glint in the eyes.

Thankyou life that my family did not witness that, the husband would have had me submitted in the mental hospital, right after Doris, and put me on the same wing as her no doubt. How does one go about discussing Kundalini? When it sounds like sexual mouth fornication? Not a sacred blessing, that those in the East are fully aware of.

Sarah thinks that Westerners yoga studios choose the practice of yoga as a flexibility work out and not as a way of surrendering to the self, merely out of fear because they are scared.

How does one living in a conditioned Western society explain feelings of electrical currents running through the body to a doctor? Of experiencing deep light energy within the crown chakra? Without full knowledge and experience, where does one turn to talk in confidence?

Sarah felt a little queasy, something within was stirring, 'Let go, let go, let go.'

Nose was following suit, just as Esther Hicks' did and running wildly, 'Observe, witness, drop it,' Sarah darling.

Sarah opened her eyes and peered down at what she had written on the Ipad: *Mooji Baba*. Incredible.

A quick search on the beloved InterWeb revealed an up and coming Satasang at one of his Silent retreats in Portugal, a week away.

What airport would Sarah fly into? Her hand flew to FARO, spelling out the letters with much enthusiasm. Sarah asked her higher self. "Are you sure you want me to go?"

YES. It tapped out. The fingers expressing their own truth.

It was time for Sarah to bathe in the presence of a Master. The higher self was directing one to truth. Something that the higher true self was desperate for.

After all, in the name of truth, Sarah had 'abandoned' her family. There was nothing...no-thing else to lose was there?

Holey moley, within a few moments, Sarah's fingers had booked a flight to Faro in Portugal and a camping place in Satasang with the Master Sri Mooji in Portugal. Her internal GPS and heart space radiated pure joy, mixed with a little side portion of nerves too. That's the voice of the divine my darling, Monkey Mind reminded me through a cheeky wink some more.

That night, it was way past 10 o'clock before Sarah went to bed. But Sarah was an independent woman now and didn't have an enquiring other half to question her whereabouts, couldn't moan at the dinner not being on the table, could go for herb tea and stay out late with her yogi pals to discuss all things conscious more deeply if she desired. Most importantly, could feel free to chat at length with the yogi students who were eager to talk about their progress, their flexibility, their feelings or their day. This gave Sarah a real buzz and opened Sarah's eyes to the realization of the 'void' or transparency in beings lives and in her own.

Nor did the yoga TTC prepare one for the richer sensitivity developed as a result, that opened Sarah up so very deeply to the connection of all beings. That we are the same source but each looking out with a different set of eyes. Holding emotions that come and go and pass like clouds, hiding the formless, the sky, the clear, pure ocean of consciousness. Carrying a sense of feeling within and without and so much more than the body. Why of course the body is skillfully crafted matter by design, incredibly intelligently so. The soul body is another incredibly, almighty powerful energy too. Gratitude for both. Sarah feels as though they are 2 separate entities working in complete harmony.

Time to settle down for the night and create clean, calming energy; the ballet pumps were neatly placed under the bed, the yogi training gear was folded away neatly in the drawer, a newly replaced pair of Om earrings were placed on the dresser, alongside a dinky rose quartz pendant necklace. Sarah lit Lit some frankincense candles and lavender joss sticks around the room, then played some soothing Moola Mantra to ease herself into a good nights deep and very beautiful sleep.

During the middle of the night a piercing screaming sound awoke a sleepy Sarah. She shot up out of bed, throwing the covers to one side, to peek behind the wooden venetian blinds to see what all the commotion was about. Now bear in mind, living so far in this holy residence, one could hear a pin drop from a distance. It was a transcendental and respectful environment.

Sleepy eyes scanned the street. The road was dimly lit with no apparent signs of a physical disturbance anywhere, only a bedroom light flickered in the house across the street?

Scratching her head, Sarah suddenly realized that she somehow could hear the voices of a heated dispute between an argumentative couple across the way, through the walls.

She, "I only wanted a hug."

He, "I am sick of your whining, leave me alone."

Or words to that effect. Sarah was a sleepy bunny. She pinched her skin.

Monkey Mind, what the fuck?

Sarah lay back down on the bed, staring up at Patzy's jazzy, retro psychedelic lampshade, no it wasn't a rotating ceiling fan but it would do.

Wow. Who could one talk to about that experience? Certainly not the family!

Before I left, the boy suggested a woodland walk and a last supper so to speak. Mum kindly accepted the offer, it was such a beautiful suggestion. Although he did think his mothers tree hugging a little bizarre and so wanted to capture the moment to share in cyber space. No chance, this was a personal, intimate sharing. An attempt for life to explain one's seemingly outwardly irrational, eccentric behaviors.

How wonderfully amazing too was his aubergine homemade lasagna. That boy possessed some serious loving kitchen Tantra. It was that tasty to the full sensory machine, Mum and the boy scoffed the whole batch. Living alone, Sarah hadn't been cooking for herself that much and had observed a rapid drop in weight, due to her sporadic pigeon eating meal times. The weight had plummeted to just under 50kg. His meal was a blessing.

However, 'nothing looks as skinny feels' and Sarah adored her new lighter flexibility and strength. Felt so much closer to God source and very aligned. Despite the mystical experiences, she felt well.

During a Skype mentorship session with her Indian Guru, he confirmed this too in suggesting, "The bodies cells are dancing, nothing to worry about." Firmly supporting these experiences as a natural process of expansion.

Though, this seems fair play in the Eastern world but in the Western? Coronation Street provides enough drama, even though Sarah had got out of that mind grasping habit a long time ago.

The trustworthy, battered 12-year relationship with the loyal Volkswagen, was coming to a very near close too. It was time to dissolve the partnership and part company on the best of terms.

A family friend knew a car mechanic who could pass it on to a new forever home, the old girl still had plenty of miles left in her yet, and Sarah was made an offer she couldn't refuse.

Time for a last lunch date with the daughter, who bravely braved the elements to come out and hook up even though she was suffering with a kidney infection.

Sarah's mother eyes could feel her pain in her hardened heart. Her Mother was lost, gone in cuckoo land. Although contrarily, Sarah felt natural and content within, the best that she had felt in a long time. It was obvious the daughter was THE attachment struggle.

Over the years, she maintained the claim that the boy was always the elder favourite child but this was in her mind not Sarah's. Every part of her feminine being was so very beautiful. God had indeed blessed one all those years ago when Sarah asked for a girl. And what a pure Goddess was delivered too. Blessed.

Gave her my deepest blessings over a nice steaming cup of soy cappuccino in our favorite little hugging café in town.

Would the daughter ever trust Mum again? Life will decide and already knows the outcome. Would she ever want to spend some quality girly Mum/daughter time some more? She hobbled off into the distance, tip lipped, Mum observed her nervously biting down on her bottom lip. That kidney infection is causing her internal pain too. "Eat plenty of watermelon," the mother voice lovingly suggested.

In daughter's eyes, Mother was a heartless bag lady, living off a whim and choosing to opt out of society. Mother felt the sickness manifesting through her kidneys. What Mother could suggest to alleviate the symptoms was far too radical for daughter to comprehend. The daughter loyally followed the advice from the doctor and spooned the antibiotics down.

In the Presence of Grace, Sri Mooji: Portugal

Bleary eyed and feeling airy, Sarah dutifully followed all the necessary passport check-in security procedures at the airport check-in desk. Passport check. The gas canisters are securely packed away in the bottom of the backpack, for the obligatory morning coffee. Check. Hugs are given to the long distance cousin for his kind lift offer at daft o'clock. Check. Well wishes are exchanged for a wondrous new experience. Check.

What did the dozy, airy Sarah do next? And only realized after clearing passport control? That she had only gone and left her ATM card in the Traveler's Exchange kiosk. She could visualize it too, her little green plastic 2D love rectangle, cheekily sticking its tongue out from a little black plastic chip and pin hole of Calcutta darkness. Drat.

What to do? Find a solution: Visualize it returning to the safe, enveloping soft, creamy pocket of said faux leatherette wallet. That's what.

The Traveler's Exchange attendant in the Departure lounge was of Indian heritage. We immediately connected and he felt my plight.

Within 11 minutes, the said lovely noun, was respectfully returned after a priority VIP escort via Passport Control. That's the simple power of life for you.

Thankyou. 2 beautiful hugs later, Sarah went off to purchase a much needed herb green tea. Monkey Mind wanted to share one too.

Destination Portugal. Very beautiful indeed, as were the universally attracted beautiful group of Shakti healers, mediums, spiritualists and yogis in the train compartment, excitedly traveling together. Destination bound: Satsang with the Master Sri Mooji.

Felt like we were aboard a locomotive steam train bound for Hogwarts, due to it's timeless anti-quainted nature.

Expectations? Drop them.

En route, the Elders openly communicated a wealth of knowledge about the Masters service. Much more so than the clueless Sarah, who had so far only watched a few of his teachings on YouTube but felt both strangely drawn to him and unsure as well. Call me a doubting Thomas, but as per usual, Sarah had to experience grace for herself.

Sat Nam Guru.

Rolling along the Mooji train to Satsang, Sarah drove the elders mad with a loop of questions, 'Rolling round the bend, now I can't see the sunshine til I don't know when but I know I had this coming, I know I can't be free.' Good old Johnny Cash. He knew too.

"BEings will burn in the fires of Ego. It is a deeply moving process. Very cathartic." The elders unanimously agreed.

Fucking hell… The stomach was churning, but very intrigued as to what the higher self had wanted Sarah to experience.

On joining the coach for the following leg of the magical mystery tour, a transparent blue, doe-eyed elfin creature informed Sarah of her preparation status. Basically, she told Sarah to, 'Shut up' with her questioning and would no further exchange any additional energetically draining communication with her. Elfin, lowered her eyelids then stared out of the window. Sarah took a long, sideways, curious glance at her thoughtfully.

A bunch of jolly looking, white robed shepherds or angels guarding the gates of heaven, couldn't decide which, greeted our beings with broad, holy smiles upon destination satsang arrival. Sarah found herself searching for Peter, I'm Peter.

What was Sarah energetically walking herself into? All felt mysterious.

Moments later, Sarah was kindly dropped off, in a minuscule golf buggy with her camping gear in tow. It wasn't long before the Masculine energy kicked in. She rolled her sleeves up, whipped the lump hammer out, lay inner and outer tent sheets flat on the floor, and before you new it…Hey presto…Job done. Complete with washing line for an added touch of Shakti homeliness. Damn it, forgot to pack any tent pegs. If only?

On returning the lump hammer to the helper's station, observed a lonely, green clothes peg embedded in the dry soil in the ground. Life you never cease to answer my requests. Thankyou, that was super speedy delivery. One was perfect enough.

Early doors pre-Satsang de-brief, confirmed the non-talk, non-eye contact, non-physical cue signs for the ensuing silent retreat. Plus, O.A.B as it cropped up. Twice each day we were to meet in an acoustic Satsang Hall for 2.5 hour Satsangs, with The Master himself elevated at the front, holding grace space. Beautiful.

This guy is a human being right? Or is he another BEing who has fallen through a hole in life? Was Jesus the same back in the day? A superior presence, able to make BEings cry or drop to their knees literally just by BEing present?

Sarah, I, she, you, he, she, it, her, Monkey Mind you are so very, very naughty. Look around and observe. Don't you feel source energy too?

It wasn't long before one realized just how much energy one wastes through verbal communication, endlessly without actual intentions.

In addition, just how powerful body language is, in fact information is energetically leaked through all the senses and how as human beings we process a multitude of energetical information through our vehicle of consciousness continually. Lest we forget. Well Sarah did. Gulp, gulp, gulp, more realization. How many times does one actually stop and think before one engages the mouth? Or covers up one's truth with unconscious actions? On how many occasions is one aware of the mind diarrhea dribbling from the mouth?

Sarah learnt sharpish, the relevance of assimilating information through clearer channels. Through feeling her way around and allowing life to flow as opposed to something that happened to her and trying to grab at it.

Sarah had definitely not lost her intuitive ability altogether, or should one reframe that to buried it, through an over saturated dense social fog.

She gets it, it is the 21st century alright, New Age philosophies can be seen as too far out and mainstream too conformist. A solution merges somewhere in the middle? One discipline is not fully comprehensive on its own accord. Rather like science and spirituality, holistic medicine versus conventional. They form a bridge to fully complement one another. Right?

Well, if the Silent Retreat didn't 'do' anything for Sarah, at least the food was a bonus. Ego mind was having an emotional ball stuffing its fat face with delicious Mediterranean salads and vegetables, such an impressive range of tastes, textures and live cells, freshly prepared with tremendous amounts of love. Sarah couldn't resist the freshly baked gluten free cakes and puddings either, the raw cacao Angel Delight was a firm favourite too.

Nothing like the English version your Mum would prepare for you as a kid with dollops of sprinkles on. However, it didn't turn Sarah into an angel, more like a hyperactive, cheeky little miss know it all, after stuffing that sweet, gooey stuff in her gob. Creating chaos for her lovely parents and torment for her little brothers and sisters...lol.

Over the next few days Sarah decided to go easy on herself. Allowing oneself to arrive, to land, to settle and familiarize ones BEing with the layout of the camp, and setting oneself a daily routine to ensure ones BEing is fully appreciative and submerged enough in the process. To be allowed to contemplate, be still, to address any emotions as and when they arose and to be perfectly present in the unfolding procedure.

'Portugal evenings get very cold, please bring extra blankets for camping.' Thankyou Mooji.org. Well how about adding to bring a hot water bottle too?

A chilly Sarah lay back in her cosy pup tent, and wrapped herself up in layers of thermals, complete with Buff, Beanie hat, fleece, coat, grannies knitted jumper, 2 pairs of thermal socks, leggings, base layer and crocheted fleece blanket. Yet again.

The ground is extremely bitter without proper insulation, although the cold became Sarah's friend after a few days bonding. However, another body to snuggle upto at night would have made her the warmest happiest.

The following morning Sarah awoke at 6a.m., bright eyed and bushy tailed, to the sweet tones of a piano melody. The Dirty Dancing ringtone had well been given the push.

Firstly, she pulled the zip down on the inner then outer tent to allow the morning sunburst and fresh air to filter through. Secondly, she whipped on some yoga trousers for 5 rounds of glorious Surya Namaskar followed by a short 31 minute asana practice. Sarah knows all to well how highly important it is to shift the energy around in the morning, as animals do. What does a dog or cat do after waking up from a nap? ...Downward facing dog...Naturally, of course! One is only as old as the spine feels!

How blessed was Sarah that she could now could work with her own body, listen it it and understand the dynamics to shift the energy around the body, especially after sleeping horizontal on a cold, hard floor all evening. On the plus side, hardness became her friend as well.

The walk to the breakfast hall was most amusing. Sarah found herself lost in an ocean of non-communicating sleepwalkers, each one happily locked into their own source of BEing walkers. One could suggest a prisoner of war camp vibe, held not on force but rather in choice alone.

How on earth hundreds and hundreds of bodies are more than suitably fed and watered and impeccably catered for, impressed Sarah. Sarah observed BEings even going up for second helpings. The food supply/demand seemed to be relentless, it just kept coming on the never ending, delicious conveyor belt of Mooji love.

Interestingly, his flock cleverly used hand written signs to keep the bodies streaming fluidly and with grace, no-one BEing was seen to be in a rush, in a hurry, impatient or experiencing the emotion of anger, as one experiences these days. One feels this everywhere; in fast food chains, in restaurants, in restroom queues, in car parking lots, you name it, unconscious BEings are in a constant rush to get somewhere, but where?

After breakfast a satisfied Sarah returned her tray to the stacking counter, by written instruction of course, then hurriedly made her way over to angelic sounds coming from the Satsang tent.

There are no words but many to describe BEing present at a live Bajans, exhilarating, majestic, uplifting, inspirational, divine...Nahh...None do it justice enough.

One has to experience and feel for oneself, the angelic vibrations transcending the air space, pulling one's energy in the vortex, deeply passionate and with incredible divine beauty; essentially, God's creative, harmonious angels, freely expressing their joy for all to share. Sarah's body felt the urge to move and dance. And not from trauma release or wanting to be or look ego sexy. This was God consciousness rhythmical moving, free to express the body of femininity through the language of hips type of dancing.

As a kid, Sarah remembers seeing such hollering folk on church TV programmes. Conditioning led one to believe that they were weird bible bashers. Now, who is the foolish one to believe that? Just another character mask, a costume one worn at the time.

Sarah now feels this...How BEings experience joy is divinely unique to them.

During Satsang, Sarah sat quietly and witnessed and observed attentively throughout. She did not feel the desire to share because the questions raised, always resonated in some form or another, confirming one's belief that yes, we all are actually one source experiencing random emotions and experience's at any time. Fuck me. This is truth. Sorry but not sorry for swearing. But until one experiences this cathartic process directly, one will not realize the fully implications. What happened to some bodies? They dropped like flies.

Lovingly, the Mooji's flock would gently nurse the body back to recovery, right there and then on the floor as it unfolded. First time Sarah observed this she so wanted to go over and help out, so very typical of her. This was not Sarah's karmic duty. She had to remain still, remain silent, listen, observe and FEEL.

Dear ones, Sarah will not go into specific details about the daily unfolding's of Satasang with the Master, out of respect, integrity and honour for universal divine intelligence.

Although Sarah will share this, Sri Mooji is an extremely beautiful being. Sarah does not know his story fully, nor needs too. Although his lovely daughter does have the same lovely biblical name as her lovely daughter, funny, lovely coincidence.

The heart feels every lovely thing.

His sheer presence alone is enough to shift your BEing into a fuller expression of self, juicily heart opening and all. Fundamentally, his powerful masculine energy is a very strong reflecting mirror, so wide and all encompassing. Dare meet yourself self?

Sarah will add that she feels this too…. Sri Mooji is a mortal man just like any other prophet long before time, like Jesus, Mohammed or Krishna, alongside many, many other Saints who lived truth.

Sarah also loved his spiel, his use of metaphors, his use of similes, his use of imagery…How can the knife cut itself...How can the eye see itself? Beautiful.

A cheeky embrace one morning after Satsang, gave Sarah the opportunity to feel his very presence, right through his bodily skin to that big, will not say old, huge encompassing vibrational heart of his, radiating so much depth and energetical source love. It felt like it could 'crush a grape,' quite literally. As 'The Crankies' would say.

Blimey, she didn't bow down to her husband, when at times she should have done, let alone to another man. No Sarah was not for idolizing false idols.

Without much fuss, The Wizard of Oz green curtain was slipping away very graciously. That is, right up until the closing fire ceremony and some more words of wisdom from the Master, which struck such a deep chord and resonated so greatly in the bodysoul. So strong, that Sarah threw her ember into the fire and set an intention never to doubt herself ever again.

That is, until one morning, whilst sitting under an acorn tree, lotus style mediating, waiting for Satsang to begin. Sarah observed the Master drive past, in his red pick up truck on his way to a healing. Sarah opened her eyes and blew him an unconscious, conscious kiss.

Then Sarah noticed something very peculiar happen, she felt as though she left her body in the lotus position, under the acorn tree, and how, don't know, just did, then found herself present at the foot of a bed of an elderly lady with crooked toenails and short greying hair, swept over gently to one side, wearing a pale blue sweater. The master was holding her hand and comforting her soothingly. She was going through a deep cathartic process.

Sarah felt very present and still, that's all. Like a calm, loving blanket sat motionless in the situation? Yet, somehow Sarah was that soft, fluffy blanket? Make sense?

After a while, maybe 10 minutes or so later, Sarah returned to her body, opened her eyes and was again sat, lotus style, under an impressive acorn tree, 1 of 5 to be exact, see how one likes counting? Lol.

Next thing you know, the elderly lady, of exact former description, scurries by, not wanting to late for Satsang. Sarah thanked life, got up and made he way up the embankment to join Satsang herself. Sarah followed crooked toes, so she could get a real view of them. Yes, for sure, they were exactly how 'my' outer soul body 'saw' them. Sarah shrugged inside, a very beautiful, smile. OM. Amen.

She took her shoes off outside the Satsang tent, still in great earshot to the Master and his disciples, just to ground herself some more. She still felt a little perplexed, a little intense after what she had just experienced and wanted/needed to rub the feet erratically on the grass and connect with nature to ground properly.

Needless to say, the morning Satsang was magically intense and it did not stop there either.

What's more, that very same evening Sarah woke from a very deep sleep to voices calling her from outside the tent. Now hang on a minute, this was a silent retreat, perhaps Sarah was hearing voices due to the lack of her spoken word? That Monkey Mind was upto his old tricks again having a little fun? Mind game warfare style?

"Sarah, Sarah," the voices softly called. She heard it twice more.

Sarah sleepily opened the tent zipper and peaked around in the dark, the campsite field was still and motionless. Absolutely no-one around. Dazed and confused, Sarah fell back down to sleep, squirreling herself for the umpteenth time her many layers, even though the cold was her friend. Just another mystical experience to witness, that all. Night, night God bless. Sweet dreams.

The light evening rain had persistently been dripping in on the tent, weighting it down on one side, the overheard pergola hadn't helped much either in protecting one from the elements, for it too had a large tear in the tarmac covering. On closer inspection, Sarah's little 4-star luxury pup tent had now had its day. It was now covered in a golden brown mulchy substance that had sprayed up the sides and would be impossible to repair.

Sarah and Co decided to leave the tent, there and then. It would be a waste of energy to take down and try to get fixed up sadly. Or to even try folding down to nothingness, to fit in a small carrycase, when enveloped in a rigor mortis clay compound and riddled with holes!

Most importantly, the French press for morning coffee, camping stove and a few clothes were packed up in the rucksack instead. That coffee press would never be abandoned. Sarah had strong noun love attachment issues with that one.

Sarah would like to also mention that whatever being is looking after her baby pink sweater that she left/lost near the outdoor swimming pool, her gorgeously sweet, favourite Topshop sweater, the one she adored wearing for yoga practice. Sarah hopes that one is enjoying the Mooji love poured into it immensely. Monkey Mind once commented that he liked me in that particular sweater too, it was a sentimental favourite. Although, noun attachments are very unhealthy for you and should come with a government warning. So pink sweater, I have let you go. On one level of awareness. On another if you have it, please return to life. With love baby pink Topshop sweater.

What next, no next. What unfolds? A crying Sarah, seemingly heart broken, sobbing profusely, lying sprawled across a double bed in a quirky, blue hotel room in Faro. Crying for God or crying for Monkey Mind? Spent 3 full days stewing, only venturing out next door to sip a smoothie when the mouth felt dry and stomach felt tight. Occasionally, popping up to the rooftop garden, to salute the sun with sunken eyes and a heavy heart.

Why? Felt really humble and focused during Satsang. Felt really mindful and conscious when washing, showering, eating and through yoga practice. Of daily intentions set to FEEL more. To give space to others to do the same. Felt pretty awesome really. Well, something felt different that Sarah was not accustomed to feeling, put it that way.

Perhaps Sarah was suffering from Mooji soup fever withdrawal? The realistic intensity only hitting home afterwards? On closure of the Mooji bubble? On the work that still needed to be done? In for a penny, in for a pound my dear Father used to say.

A forlorn Sarah sat on the end of her bed and meditated. What to do?

As if by fairy-tale, under a magical puff of smoke, a Skype conversation request popped up from a Thai Yoga Massage Therapist on the lovely isle of Koh Phanghan, Thailand. Sarah had forgotten all about sending her an email, requesting further course information a few months ago. As universal luck would have it, she had space for private tuition. Sarah wanted to develop her touch technique, to drop to the feminine principle more and be able to share it. She knew her touch was a little insensitive, unrefined and hardened slightly at times. This came as a result from surrounding her spiritual heart with layers of cast iron over the years.

Though, when the pups were little, Sarah remembers being able to express a gentle touch, when putting the baby grows on, bathing the kids with bubbles, rubbing their backs gently if they cried, purifying the food for easy digestion and tucking them in for the night after a nice story. Aww, fond memories of motherly love. Bliss.

Hey life do you know how wonderfully magnificent you are? Place what one desires in the vortex and wait for it to show up and...BINGO.. No need to run and chase it, sit back relax, it comes to you without hardly any effort. Esther Hicks you are an awesome female Shakti soul sister, bless.

Without hesitation, Sarah booked a connecting flight from Manchester to Bangkok, to travel later that evening. Such a beautiful, sweet transition. Perfect, sweet as a nut timing.

Relieved, a visa wasn't necessary for a months stay, but according to the internet there are ways of obtaining extensions, if one so desires to lengthen the stay in the country. No problems there then. Click, click, click. Booking confirmed.

Sarah wiped the tears from her eyes, paid the cute receptionist who slept behind the counter on a pop-up sofa bed, then took the bus with other noticeable Mooji-ettes, destination bound Faro airport.

On the short transfer to the airport, there was a lot of manic conversations flying around, BEings openly shared their concerns about how to return to mainstream normality? How to ease oneself back into full time work? Is this one's truth? 'My' true soul mission? Facing the, I Am within a role that creates 'my' energy/money, money/energy to serve and connect with other beings from the heart? That, I AM reasonably content and happy...clap along if you feel like a room without a roof...coz I'm happy...Make sense?

Questions, questions, questions, Sarah felt and heard them all with such empathy. Her emphatic radar was out in full effect and picking up all sorts of sensitive heart information and as per usual processing the dam lot.

Flying High in Thailand

A nonchalant, mid evening flight from a Manchester en route Bangkok, went relatively smoothly. Except for a brief encounter at the security check-in desk, over a suspected security breach. The contents of her rucksack, had alarmingly provoked suspicion. A puzzled Sarah was asked to step aside and underwent the protocol about said item. Had anyone tampered with it, packed anything in it other than her etc., etc. She scratched her head? No?

After a few moments, the offending object was found. Funnily, the camping gas canister bottle that had somehow managed to 'slip' through customs into Portugal, was in fact a potential threat to the airline. Due to the latent explosive dynamics of the container if placed under the luggage hold of the airline. Sarah was definitely not a terrorist and reassured the non laughing airport security check guy. Note to self, certainly not a time for jokes, silly woman, get a grip. Apologies given. Said item confiscated. Hope they cooked on gas in Thailand. Sarah really needed her 'smack my bitch up' coffee fix in the morning. She then made her way through to the departure lounge, ready or not ready, certain but not certain of her following unfolding by life. Welcoming the number 8's flashing up in succession at jewelers stands, at cosmetic counters and on the coffee table counters. This was a good sign from the angels.

Once more, life blessed Sarah with more remarkable travelling companions along the way.

On the first leg of the trip, Sarah encountered a gorgeous Crystal Child; a 22-year American boy from the deep South, fittingly named Parker. Who at first and rather nervously, chatted the usual polite civilities, until Sarah noted a shift in linguistics and then the words flowed most naturally from the heart space. Sarah could feel this boys huge, enormous heart.

So, Sarah had indeed internalized understanding from Satsang with the Master. This was becoming obvious and unfolding naturally. Wow. Sarah had no control either, it was just flowing so very beautifully. She was always a quick learner.

The conversation took a natural discourse covering several topics including spirituality, connections and desires.

However, his main issue was his boredom with alcohol. This big boy could drink and had the body weight and mass to prove it. All 6 foot 4 inches of him and possibly carrying a hulking frame of at least 123kg. What a pair. Little and Large.

More over, he looked like he could do with 2 seats, with his hips squished in the tiny airline leatherette arm rests. This giant also looked like he needed 2 airline meals to fill him up as the trays came around, which looked like doll size portions in his shovel like, very masculine, beautiful hands. Sarah offered him her bread rolls and muffin which he gracefully accepted. Once a mother feeder always a mother feeder.

Sarah felt proud of this young boy's commitment to his soul wants, having a boy of similar age and wanting the same experience for growth, really resonated well with her.

Impressively, against his family and girlfriends wishes, Parker, the middle child of 6 kids, decided upon his self to listen to an inner calling. To travel to a country that he had never visited before, that he did not know about properly, or the language or cultural traditions. Only what he had read from the internet and little phrase books. "Erm, yes, I think asking where to buy condoms will be very useful in Thai language. One never Knows, it may crop up."

We fell about laughing and shared some more abstract phrases.

Simply put, he felt the deepest need to offer his services on a 6-week charity programme. To where, he did not know but he was being collected safely from the airport. Nor could Parker pronounce the name of this area in the North of Thailand. His heart just took him there for much needed expansion and growth.

More signs of trust in life. Love it. Isn't this the very intention of our majestic life? Another notch on the bedpost in support of this universal love force and connection. How much more proof did Sarah need?

The darling Parker came to find Sarah after luggage collection. He shook my hand with his great big warm paw and said that he would never forget me. His big, wide open, juicy heart transmitting love flowed threw the handshake, up my arm and into the heart and head space. A beautiful, brief exchange on the walkalator.

But guess what Parker. I didn't tell you that I would not forget you either. At how you touched Sarah's soul with your very natural beautiful intentions. No doubt, life blessed you with everything you needed to absorb in your 6-week voluntary, charity programme. Suffering is grace too. Remember that. Bon voyage angel.

Sarah arrived in a frantic Bangkok, late in the evening. Blimey, the place was a concrete jungle, of swarming bee beings, crisscrossing one another hap hazardly, trying to get to this way or that.

Sarah had never been in such a huge airport before and felt insignificantly lost and weighted down with an enormous backpack on, which was larger than her. Wobbling there alone, trolley dolly in hand, clueless in another.

Monkey Mind pops up, "What now?"

"How on earth does one get to Koh Phanghan from here?" Quizzed Sarah.

Life help!

Eyes were feeling very heavy from the night flight, the belly was feeling famished, yet excited and confused.com all at the same time.

A passing attendant, pointed one in the direction of Bangkok Airlines. A tired Sarah had to navigate her way up several escalators, and got jam sandwiched in between Turkish and Russian backpackers. She felt the heat rising in her belly. Monkey Mind offered another unwanted suggestion at this hour. He was silenced immediately.

"What is the time of the next flight to Samui please?" Sarah sleepily enquired as she made her way into a tiny but empty airline kiosk, staffed by 2 glam Thai dolls.

She had decided not to stay overnight at the Bangkok Holiday Inn, even though it was visibly prominent from the arrivals lounge and looked a safe option for a lone, female traveller at that hour. Far better than travelling into Bangkok city so late anyway.

Plus, Sarah had heard so many contradicting stories about the city that she felt uncertain braving it alone anyway.

From research carried out on the trusty InterWeb, suggested the whiskey a go-go neon lights did not lure gold, but seemed to disguise a wild city of debauchery. The nighttime had yet to become her friend fully.

No, Sarah would take a late night connecting flight to Samui and find a hotel there to rest before the onward boat trip to the idyllic, mystical island of Koh Phanghan.

"One moment please, madam," pristine air flight stewardess checks screen.

"Next flight, right now, 4000 Baht," stammers a very drunken, beefy Scottish guy, as he slams down a fistful of Thai currency on the counter, while pushing through the door and barging straight in front of Sarah.

Oh dear, something deep within Sarah felt immediately un-aligned. What had the universal cat dragged in? Her stomach felt even queasy, but why?

The negative energy exuding him, dripped anger, contempt and downright bullish ways. His breath sadly stank of many toxins, of nicotine, whiskey, lager, pain and regret. This was a late situation for Sarah to deal with so she quickly paid for her connecting flight then made her way to the bar area to collect a bottle of water.

Be prepared Sarah girl, look after yourself, this light aircraft may not offer refreshments and by the time you arrive in Samui, it will be quite late, past midnight even, where does one purchase provisions at that hour? Most hotel lobbies are closed. Monkey Mind warbled on.

The next minute, toxin man was sat at the bar next to me, ordering a pint of lager and several whiskey chasers. Sarah cringed.

What you think more of, you will attract. Sarah tried really hard to advert the situation. She closed her eyes momentarily and wished him lots of love, to heal his painful heart.

Sarah must have been sleepy and lacking intention because this time, toxins man's energy was overly powerful, grasping at hers.

A sudden intercom announcement interrupted her thought processing, at which she jumped up in search of Departure Gate 7. Toxin man fast on the heels. He was heading in the same direction and taking the same flight. Oh shit.

Through drunken slur, this guy conveyed something else as he angrily ranted on about his dissatisfactions with life, before fiercely unclipping his belt for security. This made Sarah wince.

Monkey Mind suggested that this guy was a potential rapist or torturer of some sort? Sarah really needed to get away from this negative energy. She climbed aboard the small awaiting aircraft and without fuss, sat in quietly in a window seat, lowered her eyelids as though asleep.

What next, this big, wobbly, half cut oaf, plonks himself down in the seat right next to her and picks up the conversation left at the bar. Throwing in an invitation to stay at his house as a guest upon arrival in Samui. And what a brave girl I was to be travelling all alone in the country at that hour. Patronizing git.

Not forgetting to mention his generous heart, and his drunken talk of day trips to waterparks with young, disadvantaged Thai kids. What a hero.

This guy worked on the oil rigs part way in the year and part lived on the island for the rest. What a colourful story. One that Sarah did not need or want to listen to any further.

Sarah declined and went back to her pretend sleep, meditating on loving kindness, to permeate this mans rotten story. God bless him, she thought.

Unfortunately, he just wouldn't be told or take no for an answer. Sarah placed a finger on her lips and silenced him with a very discerning glance.

As the flight touched down smoothly into a small shanti hanger, Sarah quickly latched herself onto an English-speaking honeymoon couple. Briefly updating the wife in the toilet cubicle of her distrust of the pacing toxin man, hovering up and down outside the luggage reclaim conveyor belt. Sarah could see him scratching his head. He would not intimidate Sarah any longer. Sarah waited in the toilets until she spied a chance to exit, then jumped in a mini cab, alongside several others, and requested a hotel to the driver.

As she got in, she heaved a huge sigh of relief. She had escaped the wrath of the drunken, intimidating toxin man. She felt a new feeling of safety.

Now, this was placing trust in life; certainty in the knowledge of finding a decent place to stay for the evening, way past midnight and on a small, sleepy unfamiliar island with no Thai language knowledge.

Sarah had never travelled to Asia before so had no expectations of the island or its culture either. Nor could she claim to be an experienced traveller. More like a Brit on tour as a rabbit caught in headlights. She explained her needs as best she could to the taxi driver.

One by one, beings were dropped of to their respective hotels. The helpful taxi driver, stopping to enquire if there was any extra availability for me, none yet. Understanding body language here and not fluent Thai of course.

Eventually, one hotel worker had a vacancy and scribbled the price of a nights stay down on paper. Over 100 Great British Pounds. That was expensive and wasn't worth the price, considering such an early a.m. start. Declined the offer kindly, and asked the driver in best my best broken English to find a cheaper one. So off we went, back tracked our way down a deserted side street, made several turns to a deserted car park with and a few barren palm trees, in view of the beach and imminent sea shore. Nothing else.

Sarah's heart began to race. Shit, was her physical body about to get raped? She was the only female in the 7-seater mini bus left. He had taken her to a dead end, no-one was about. The evening just seemed to get weirder and weirder. What was she attracting and not letting go of?

Doris had drummed into child Sarah to always be fearful of the dark, of men, of being alone and putting oneself in compromising situations. Hadn't all these apparent fears all become my friends now? Hadn't she shown life how well she had done so far? How had Sarah attracted more negativity vibrationally?

"Flery, flery, you take morning flery from here," reassured taxi man driver as if sensing the sudden fear.

Sarah you daft fool, trust all is well, this guy is genuine. He was only showing you where to catch ferry from in the morning.

He started the engine up and took a few more left and right turns. This wonderful Thai guy, with charming broken English, took Sarah to a cheaper overnight hotel, literally 5-mins walking distance from ferry port.

Thai yoga massage therapy course, here Sarah comes. Next new experience. Thankyou.

Sarah slept soundly for the next several hours, rolling around in white sheets like a tuna fish trapped in a net, only this was a trapping in a four poster. Did her dream state bring up her insecurities from her previous evenings late night encounters? Was this a warning shot fired from the good old life to be more present, to think more good thoughts, to send more love? Who knew what was released in that deep unconscious state. Certainly, not bad pickings for a cheap, late night hotel, half the price of the others, she remembered somewhere in her short term memory field containing a wild hallucination from the night beforehand.

Graciously naked, Sarah slipped out of her elegant pit, slid over to the power shower to awaken her body under refreshing jets of warmth, carefully balancing the feet steady on the hard, firm neutral elements. Setting too, the intention for the day to be firm and steady as well, ready to be witness or awareness, perceived or perceiver which ever floats your Thai boat.

Donning her yogi clothing, in balance with the jet set backpacking travelling crew observed so far, Sarah made her way down to the poolside snack bar for a quick bite to eat before a short stroll to catch the 7am ferry, to the last leg of the trip.

Observing closely, for the first time, the elegant softness of the pretty scenery. Watching the shore gently lap, whist mindfully nourishing the body's cells with juicy fruits of the land. Some of which, I didn't know what they were as they were cut into tiny, ornate petals or umbrellas or something else very artistic. Something Asian people seem to be very good at, manipulating nouns to create a wonderful image, whether it be with food or carefully crafted towel on the bed, displaying a cute elephant or gracious welcoming swan or something similar. A skill admired by many but impatience never allowing to get it right. Sarah should know, her party trick with a napkin was not a sight to behold. Not worth leaving on a bed to welcome guests that's for sure, more akin to something one could wipe their bottom on and flush away.

The short ferry ride across the peaceful ocean, remained true to the start of the day, tranquil and idyllic. Noting little fishing boats in the distance and several little flying fish jumping out of the water, as a ferry load of excited, anxious beings were transported across also. The majority of travellers seemed to a lot younger than Sarah and in full anticipation of a big booming full moon party.

For certain, Sarah had heard stories about these parties, from family and friends, but was something that did not resonate with her fully. She was here with no expectations but with many at the same time. Her focus was to develop her touch, desensitize her masculine energy, more in favour of using and applying this service for the benefit of healing others. No hedonistic full moon parties for her. Her drug fuelled dancing days, belonged way back in another story. Long ago.

Furthermore, Sarah enjoyed her prana rich lifestyle these days and couldn't see a path otherwise.

Monkey Mind was finally given the push too. Right there and then on that little ferry taxi ride across the ocean. Sarah did not want to hear his grasping egoic remarks any longer. It was time for them to part company. This next part of the journey would be Hans Solo. Sarah wanted to know if she could manage by herself, trust and surrender to life, see what it threw up without the grasping mind or manifestation of anything. Just pure unfolding. Now this was a challenge she accepted to herself as she lugged off her weighty backpack, across the little boarding plank over to the other side, to the magical island of Koh Phanghan, were dreams made of strawberry lemonade came true.

As she looked around for transportation, a thought popped up, at how big and powerful this manifesting business was. Seemed as though everyone had been doing it and for very long time, since the beginning of time even. Whether consciously or unconsciously. Sarah definitely knew which category she fell into before. What rock had she been living under too?

Just then, a taxi moped driver pulled up complete with luminous pink tabard on.

"You want ride?" In his bestest broken English accent he politely asked de-embarking tourists. Sarah waved him over, then handed him a slip of paper with an unpronounceable address on.

Cocking the leg over, she jumped on the back of the bike.

The driver took the rucksack between his legs, steadying himself on the scooter. Sarah had her trolley, dolly nestled between him and her, as a wedge of separation. It's a fine line balancing act between juggler and driver combination one mused.

She passed him the address of the therapy centre again, revved up, then set off into the sunset, laughing her head off all the way along the twist and turns of the bumpy, jungle roads. If only her kids could see her now! Lol.

When she was younger, she didn't crack eggs on her head for no reason. Attention seeking diva, more lol.

The Health and safety chiefs back in the UK would have a whopping field day, one mused further.

After about 20 minutes of hysteria, we rocked up, sandy, ruddy faced and pumping with high energy. The welcoming look, on the massage therapist face, was priceless. Fair play to the scooter driver, he never lost balance once, even through undignified snorts of piggy laughter. Sarah gave the kind man a hefty tip.

The pre-booked apartment was a complete dream. Everything a yogi could need and ask for. A beautiful little, cream bungalow, stacked up on wooden stilts with under parking for vehicles, washing lines, storage etc. Set back off the road, amidst a tropical garden of bananas trees, exotic colourful plants and green shrubbery. Fully fitted with a basic kitchen, complete with gas hob. That's the coffee press situation sorted out then she thankfully thought. A fully working, power shower, rather tepid by Sarah's standards though and a huge king-size bed and white cotton crisp bedding with plenty of light streaming in from the patio doors and offering plenty of space for self yoga practice on the balcony, next to a sturdy table, perfect for writing on and observing the passing trade, immediately thought Sarah. The Wi-Fi connection was very good to, should she need hook up with the Monkey Mind or the dear kids, so as to check on their well being? What Motherly love. Thanks to good old, strong, high vibration internet.

Sarah hooked up the very next morning with her Thai Yoga Massage Therapist, after only a short stroll to the centre, unable to consume anything but her dear coffee intake as the weather was deliciously humid and averted one's appetite.

Sarah was feeling a little bit jet lagged and couldn't focus on the Sen line of the body, just couldn't feel them or get them right much to the annoyance of her tutor.

"Press, you do like this, 70, 80, 90 relaxxx," she purred like an Asian feline pedigree cat.

Sarah's heavy hand just could not feel anything. A body underneath her touch, just felt anatomically like a piece of meat body. Nothing more. She couldn't feel what she could. This was an ancient form of healing, a very special technique. What had she gotten herself into again?

Well at the time is sounded like a god idea. Learn Ancient Patanjali Hatha Yoga principles in Holy City of Rishikesh and Ancient Thai yoga massage therapy in Thailand? Who wouldn't?

My 1:1 tutorship was going down like the titanic very slowly. Sarah buck up, wake up. Concentrate, feel, connect. My poor tutors body was feeling the pain of my touch, plus, the I am presence, felt that this Shakti Asian Goddess was starting to get annoyed at her decision to be the dummy for learning purposes.

Eventually after a few days acclimatization and practice, Sarah started to get into the flow and act of giving and receiving. In being able to feel the body more sensitively, even in the tiny little forgotten nooks and crannies that hold tension and discomfort. Sarah started to get into the stream and accept her latest self challenge wholeheartedly. Mind held the constraints that this skill was impossible, that learning the art of touch as therapy to feel one's way around a human body actually existed.

So much so that eventually she got that excited and offered her service free of charge to others, to practice on.

One late evening after Massage class, Sarah went home for meditation and self practice. Just in a pair of small panties mind as the weather was so very hot and the air conditioning a little bit too intense and blowy for still, asana work. So what did Sarah do this time? Went out onto the small balcony to rinse her pants, in the wash bucket outside, when the internal door banged shut, leaving Sarah alone on the elevated balcony minus any clothes, in darkness and with no surrounding neighbours to come to her aid. Oh boy, life this was a tough one. What next...a quick scan of the area and Sarah observed a wire coat hanger that she had used formerly to hang out her t-shirt, so she unraveled that with precision then fed it threw a mesh window guard, very carefully, to hook the door key which was favorably lying on the kitchen worktop. As a kid, our Dad used to take us to the funfair to play hook a duck, which Sarah used to love, receiving even the tackiest prize. This was no different, only the prize was entrance into her temporary, beautiful Tenko base.

Holding her breath, she fed the cable, very carefully. It took several attempts and making a bigger dent in the window guard than anticipated. However, finally the keys were in grasp. Hahaha, she felt smug as, took the keys and shoved them in the lock.

No joy, they didn't work from the outside. What type of keys only do that? Thai keys obviously.

Next risk assessment. A thick, blue rope hung from off the palm tree about a metre from the apartment. Sarah unhooked it, lent on the rickety wooden handrail, naked of course, then swung its length around the handrail several times, then observed just enough to drop to the grass floor below, about a 10 metre drop. Okay, commando style Sarah could do this. Bum cheeks in the air, balancing carefully on the ledge, Sarah took one last cry for help before taking a camacarsie leap of faith over the balcony.

When suddenly, she stopped in her racks. She magically heard her next door neighbour Tatiana's moped engine fly in, for a brief return home to collect something. Sarah knew the sound distinctly and began to cry for help. As fast as thunderbolt lightening, Tatiana came around the back to see 'me' in all 'my' naked glory. Well, her face was a picture, it glowed, that's when Sarah first noticed her eyes. Very shiny. Her skin? Very glowy. She was smiling profusely at the situation but calmly walked up the stairs, threw open the unlocked patio door and came threw the kitchen door to open this kitchen safety door, like a heavenly angel. Sarah was so thankful she offered her a free full body massage in exchange and deep appreciation.

"Thankyou, swing by tomorrow at 2pm, you can use my body then," she winked.

Sarah noted her size 7 feet, then looked at her own tiny hand span of size 3. This was going to be an interesting session. Strength, manipulation, force, gravity, tender loving care or deep painful pressure? One would find out her preferred style tomorrow. Let's see.

Sarah was more than happy to take a shower and retire to bed that night. Enough excitement and adventure was experienced for one day. Thankyou life.

A super routine followed over the next few weeks on the magical island of Koh Phanghan. Days usually flowed with: coffee, morning practice, massage, meditation, a short run along the shoreline, a short moped ride to the local markets for fresh coconut milk, fresh herbs, vegetables and other tasty fruits, all ridiculously cheap and so organic, unlike the usual supermarket wax preserved, GMO artificial substitutes in UK. In short, every delicious thing.

One time, it was hilarious balancing a drum of water and several watermelons on the scooter on the way back from the markets, dodging sandy pot holes and wet tide marks. This was a real hoot. True to form, nothing was damaged or injured in the process, just on the return parking under the bungalow stilts did Sarah rev a little bit too hard on the wet grass and flew into the wall underneath. A little bit too close for comfort but still nothing fell off. Maybe one should get a job as a taxi moped rider, she thought, or maybe in a previous life she was! Lol.

Luckily she only came off the bike a few times, quite nastily, once on a mountain bike too, taking a chunk out of her knee on a jungle trail but this was fine, a kind Thai lady helped dress the wound. Another time, falling off the moped after a heavy monsoon flood and mixed with the slippy sand and caused the roads chaos. Sarah took a corner way too fast and skidded off the bike, one leg supporting the fallen frame, bent and dripping with blood from the shattered wing mirror. She was a brave girl and didn't cry though Dad.

Great she thought. However, generous male passersby stopped to help. One tried to kick start the bike. It was having none of it. The other, motioned me to get on the back of his bike and the pair of them took me on a tour of Thai roads that Sarah had not been on before, sightseeing little back streets that opened up into long, windy roads. Witnessing idyllic scenery, beautiful.

Trust in life my dear, they feel ok, with nice helpful energy. And they did too. They took me to their repair shop and had the offending mirror repaired. Its all about the Thai Baht in Thailand, it speaks volumes.

Sarah got on the bike, even though she was a little bit shaken up by it now and its energetic cutting out and temporary inconsistent behavior. Time to take this mickey mouse bike back to the hire shop. No wonder the owner suggested on wearing a helmet at all times. He knew the temperamentally of this bike, well it probably suited a temperamental, English Hells Angel wannabe too!

Sarah had never ridden a bike alone upto that point. Never in her 40+ years. So you see folks, this was element ticked off on her to do bucket list. When one overcomes 'fear' with action. It's surprising how much one wants to do it again and again, more and more. Do not be afraid, is written in the bible 365 times, it is a daily reminder from God to live every day fearless. Sarah should know from her teaching primary school education. So very true.

After a beautiful mornings meditation, lazing on a bamboo rafter floating out in the calm ocean, sat in the presence of diving sea birds and in the distance feeling the still of the fishermen, knee deep in waders and triangular straw hats, feeling only the motion of the waves gently lapping as the sun gently rose in the sky. Sarah felt happy. After a little while, she jumped into the now rising tide and waded back home for lunch. Immediately snagging her favourite new yogi trousers on a bamboo plinth, salvaged from a 50p recycle unit. Bumcheeks. Feeling gutted en route sauntering home, noted an abundant cargo of open top jeep taxis bringing in lots of new age spiritual seekers, complete with bandanas, peace jewelry and flowing skirts and the long haired brigade in tow. More beings rocking up for the full moon party thought Sarah. Bliss.

Envision the type. Yeah man, far out, we just wanna sit on a rock and meditate dude, feel the energy vibe thing man. Oh bloody hell. They even had ego, reflecting mirror Ray Ban sunglasses on. Was this their ego trip? Who was even thinking this or even discerning this man?

Needless to say, Sarah felt the energy get darker. Otherwise chilled out, the dogs started running up and down wildly barking at the constant influx of seekers, ready to party on the the other side of the island luckily.

More so, as the full moon night approached, the beat of the drums seemed to summon a mysterious energy. Sarah did not like it and stayed indoors meditating.

Kindly refusing an invitation with Cleopatra, or Mary and Josephs wife, of a former life, to go to the beach for a late night magic mushroom experience. Declined with grace. The eyesight wasn't great in the dark. Sarah was only riding the moped in day light hours, this was a priority to keep the body safe. Sarah was daft enough in the daylight. Her Dad's pet nickname for her wasn't Head-The-Ball for nothing!

What unfolded? This divine feminine Shakti Goddess, came to the bungalow instead, to heal Sarah's poor eyesight. She would try anything to rid the face of the glasses. Incidentally, the session went rather well too; regressing back to the time in childhood, when the initial eyesight began to deteriorate and she lovingly sent lots of juicy love to each and every phase of the increasing visual impairment. It was fun also. This healing queen had a very powerful energy, especially when she stripped naked for a shower and shouted, "Fuck you!" across the quadrant in the direction of my landlord, an ex Thai cop.

Who on a daily basis, and growing with intent, would greet me with, 'Electri, electri, leave light on, fan on," in his best broken English. Sarah also knew to jot down the meter reading so that he couldn't rip her off at the end of the rental agreement as well. She found the electric box at the back of the property and prized it open, smart arse. Well she wasn't brought up in the lovely city of Loverpool for nothing and she was her Daddy's girl after all.

If you can't beat 'em, join 'em and be one step ahead of the game. His famous last words. Well some of them. Bless.

During a leisurely, could have been a Sunday afternoon, moped ride through the twisting, thin and narrow jungle roads, out to find a gentle flow Hatha class, less orientated with the Kundalini experience. Sarah became overwhelmed by the different scented aromas she absorbed along the way, delivered by the wind, laden with delicious smells and sweet, light edible fragrances.

A hidden gem to surrender, to service the body was eventually found, by a hot and sweaty sticky Sarah, who really desired a steam room cleansing and purification and certainly after a long, sandy trek up hill through the mountains.

Such was most welcomed by a beautiful couple, organic and full of integrity who ran the centre for many a year. Sarah was a happy bunny.

On her slow, sweeping drive back, feeling relaxed, in alignment with the body, Sarah stopped of at Agama Yoga Centre by default en route. She got off her scooter, parking it up rather erratically, in the parking lot, nearly taking out several bikes at the time. Dam those brakes and wet floor.

She had heard of this yoga school before but never had actually experienced it for herself. It seemed shrouded in mystical, undisclosed ambiguities. What was so special about this yoga school that everyone on the island seemed so fascinated with, yet reluctant to talk about? Sarah's open self was as ever curious. Naive too.

So what did she do? Look on the notice board for the yoga timetable, chatted with a really helpful receptionist about several interested courses for self development. Asked about several healing programmes and was instructed to visit another office not far away for advice. This was good. All is perfect.

Sarah set her intention to come return later that evening to participate in a hatha yoga and mediation class. Beautiful.

She glanced at her watch, time for another magical, mystery tour to an unknown jungle residence, to meet yet another very present being who seemed to have fallen threw the hole in life too, in Sarah's eyes anyways, so to speak.

Another slippery trek in sandy dirt tracks, and no Sarah just couldn't get used to the sensitivity of the brakes on the bike. On pressing the brakes to stop, the bike accelerated forward, with furious intention, and visa versa. Strange?

Eventually, she made her way to a secret meeting with other like minded conscious beings, also in search of truth. Then amusingly, found herself in a little convoy of mopeds, like a Vespa Brighton Scooter Rally, very rock and roll.

In a hurry, laterally launching oneself off the bike on arrival to the elevated jungle shanti shanti wooden hut, as the wheels carried on spinning around and around on the floor, as if in agony yet thankful that this dam crazy, middle aged woman had got off!

Sarah ran up the wooden plank staircase, full of intrigue and wonder as to the unfolding of the meeting: A quirky little bijou, heartcircle gathering, cross legged seated on vibrant cushions on beech, supporting floorboards, protected from the sun rays, with billowing sheets of off white netting that cascaded from the beams above.

As ever, teacher mode in full effect and hardly backward in coming forward because she liked the sound of her own voice! Sarah didn't hesitate to speak or ask questions when the video camera started rolling. Did one feel empathy as the tears rolled down the cheeks of some sensitive beings, struggling in their own body? As one by one beings shared deeply from the open heart space?

Yes, one wanted to reach out and hug them all, but from experience Sarah had realized that some stories are not part of one's karmic journey, so resolved to stay true to her own path of truth instead and simply listened, observed and rested in the being of the I am presence alone.

What had unfolded here? That spirituality is under a revamp. To witness and observe is so 2014. 2015 is all about expectations and purifications.

What had started to happen in Sarah's world? Did she see 'cracks' appearing in the world of spirituality?

It had started to become apparent that many masters and beings were essentially hooking up to the same truth, but shared rather different expressions of it.

What did Sarah feel, what did Sarah believe, to be aligned with her? Good question?

During dinner, a few evenings previously, Sarah had been involved in a topic of conversation with regards to healing trauma from the body which included making love with a variety of beings in different ratios. Plus, other varying suggestions.

Whatever served the higher purpose, in the name of Tantra, from a place of love, was fine. Tantra is not what the West preconceive, as published by the likes of the Karma Sutra. Indeed, not, Tantra is an expression of love, in every shape and form. Sarah should know, she had been introduced to this concept initially from the Hridaya Priestess in the lovely city of Loverpool and had since been reading around on the subject further for more wisdom.

In the UK strangely, we have just 1 word for love. In the East, Sanskrit has 96 definitions of this little word. So dear ones, cooking together, sharing, bathing, talking, walking, laughing, crying, dying, helping, giving, receiving etc. etc., one get's the picture? All different expressions of the same source of love, our being, our nature.

Firstly, Sarah had experienced the body and its cathartic healing process with her guru in Spain and India. However, she still felt a heavy feeling in her heart and sacral chakra, no matter how many Camel poses or back bends she did to 'open the heart' she sill felt closed in relation to being. Neither had she mastered drawing the energy up through the process of sublimation.

What did life suggest? Of should one reframe bring to her, sweetly on her doorstep complete with fresh coconut and straw one morning after Agama yoga practice? The most beautiful, big hearted, extremely present being, with such a caring masculine sensitive disposition.

"Ok, now Sarah, why do you want this type of sacred massage?" Sensitively enquired this very beautiful Soulmale.

"Well..." Sarah went on as women do and for about the next half hour, about how she really felt; after childbirth, during her marriage as a multi-tasking Shiva woman, about the problems she had to communicate exactly what she wanted during love making. Such like.

Soulmale listened intently and never took his beautiful eyes of her during the whole conversation, apart from to look at how she held her body, sipped her coconut milk shyly from the straw like little girl, or pick up on any little tell tale give away signs to help him understand her desires.

Sarah knew she was in safe hands immediately and arranged to meet for this sacred form of massage therapy the very next day. Keen not to waste an opportunity for expansion and feel the self through the loving support of life.

What a way to realization she thought. A big Thanks to life.

On the drive back to the apartment, Sarah also thought of the precious daughter. Maybe when she gets older she will have the urge to walk a path too? Maybe she will come upon the sacred yoni massage also?

Sarah had to experience this form of intimate massage for herself so that she could pass on knowledge to others. And not be short changed by an imposter, claiming to heal. There are gratifying energy vampires out there desperate to get their hands on the sacred spot. Sorry but not sorry, they are about, serving their own karmic purpose. Nonetheless, Sarah has to share.

Some women in todays society have forgotten just how sacred this place is on female form. It is a God given blessing, engineered to the highest degree to give the highest form of energy which should be shared only with integrity and honor.

How many women, or men for that matter, after casual sex, or non-consensual sex, suffer from incredible mixed deep feelings of pain after such mindless encounters? Regrettably, in the carnal act, DNA cells have been shared but alchemically or from the big, fat, juicy heart or with love intentions in the first place.

This is very special but straight forward knowledge; honor the seed that nourishes the flower, that spreads, grows and cultivates in abundance with fully fledged consciousness and awareness blessings.

Sarah couldn't wait to get to sleep that night and rigorously followed the instructions the next morning not to eat but drink plenty of water, shower and clean shave the delicate areas underneath.

It was Sarah's turn this morning to wake up with the full melodic symphonies of a piano orchestra, name unknown, sourced via YouTube, which gave Tatianna a run for her money as usually, her sweet divine feminine self would play some beautiful, soft melody to greet the day that filled the air with joy.

Excitedly, Sarah jumped on her rickety, scooter and headed off for her appointment with Soulmale to a secret jungle location, high in the mountains hidden under a canopy full of tweeting, colourful green and yellow wings of paradise.

Without hesitation, she made her way up the tracks to a most delightful looking treehouse, designed in true Thai style, of thick, wooden construction, dark red, Eastern tapestry rugs, cushions and throw overs, sweeping voiles to keep out the mosquitoes and low futon style lounge chairs.

The ceremony began very formerly. The intentions were beautifully set, whilst soft music played in the background. Soulmale and I sat opposite one another, in the lotus position, drawing in each others presence as the sacred ceremony began. Soulmale washed his hands, retrieved the coconut oil as Sarah very carefully removed her clothes; her cut off denims, her white t-shirt and glasses and folded them very neatly in a pile at her side.

Under some circumstances, some women have been known to throw each item of clothing off in a blind rage. Each woman is a unique, beautiful individual flower with one's own story to tell. One cannot suggest what serves you. It is a private matter of internal womb healing. The womb holds many secrets over the years, a conscious woman will know what she must do to heal.

Anyway, she slipped under a thin, cotton sheet, closed her eyes and lay down on the firm massage mattress to surrender and feel her beautiful God self. The sacred, sensual Goddess life force within, had been trapped inside for far too long. It was time to let her out, to get out of her head and into the body fuller.

The most beautiful, very present hands, very lovingly swept across the ankles, the calves, the thighs, the hips, the chest and the collar bones. Wow, Sarah didn't know that her collar bones were that sensitive to touch and an electrifying, penetrating current pulsated through the body down to the toes.

After several, very beautiful hours, she felt that sweet, loving nectar light up her juicy heart and brain.

Needless to say, Sarah will share no more of this very beautiful morning spent, in divine bliss with this incredible Soulmale. The intimate details of which, are far too sacred to share.

However, to conclude, the closing ritual was an emotional, happy and liberating one. An honorable parting of ways followed, with a deep shared understanding of the power of consciousness on a very beautiful, personal level.

Soulmale you are awesome. No doubt many females have repeated this mantra to you over the years. God bless you and I AM so happy that your incredible being graced my vortex, for just a little while. Much love.

Sarah felt light, airy and most alive for the following days to come. Her yoga and massage practice intensified, her meditation grew more defined, it was far easier to slip into that special place, where one does not want to leave from as the connection felt so imposing.

Sarah was feeling incredible, with a fresh new sense of honor and clarity and integrity. If her relationship with her husband were to be rekindled, there would have to be a lot of new learning and growth to take place, plus with a private space to do so in. Unless it was lost forever. In which case, Sarah would take her blessings for the wonderful children he had given her and the years of support and comfort they shared.

Something else cropped up. She also felt another thing. No being would enter her sacred church, unless invited to do so at life's request and for the sake of divine humanity.

Before the end of her course, Sarah needed just few more bodies to practice on in order to be proficient in the Ancient Art of Thai Yoga Massage Therapy and receive certification. Local Thai lady, model Fenn, really liked the pain that I endured on her but teacher thought that she had experienced enough.

Relatedly, Northern Goddess lass, formerly Cleopatra or Mary or Joseph's wife had rocked up at the centre a few days earlier, complete with green algae facemask on looking like a tad alien, her curly afro hair standing up in the breeze as she waltzed in life-size through the doors, searching for hands on healing. Beautifully hilarious.

Nevertheless, Sarah obliged, this was a good experience for her to feel the contrast in a slender, delicate body, adding to her repertoire of a Thai body, a thick set heavy body, a soft female body and a hard, muscular definition of a male body.

This catalogue of energy bodies suggested some revealing factors. One size does not fit all and the power of intention of feeling must be respectfully tuned into before hand, before touch, before exploration.

Sarah had gotten into the habit of meditating with her 'willing subjects' to balance the energy before any body work took place. This was a great way to stabilize energies.

One has to be respectful of one's story or experiences that one has endured. One has to be very mindful of that, to allow the reciprocal flow of energy healing to be exchanged with blessings.

Sarah was deep in contemplation and decided to go for a swimsteam, to an Organic Healing Centre a few Baht's around the corner, for a refreshing swim in a saltwater pool and chill in herbal steam spa. Sarah fancied joining a yoga class and got chatting to the newly appointed Manager there, Mo, whilst splashing up and down the lengths of the pool and admiring the fuchsia pink flowers on show.

An immediate connection was established. Within the space of a few, short minutes, brief introduction and small talk over with.
This tall, dark and handsome young guy was only a few years older than her boy. Yet, he appeared a very old soul, very spiritual, passionate and dedicated to his Allah and prophet Mohammed, peace be upon him.
Right from the start one had set an intention of rescuing him, a boy and a son like figure with strong Islamic beliefs. It was clear he was going through an internal battle and conflict himself. Naturally, Sarah wanted to help and invited him to her place for some hands on healing body work. This was her nature.
For him, a free massage would benefit his stress levels as his new line of work was out of alignment for him, offering an abundance of challenges and opportunities for enquiry at incredible speed. He too was still relatively wet behind the ears from the UK and transitioning into the Thai culture, which was a very steep, intense learning curve. Least never having experienced the Asian culture before, least as a Muslim in a predominantly Buddhist community.

What a pleasant, unexpected friendly exchange, one considered, as we sat together practicing pranayama in the busy steam room. Mo offered a trade. He was quick to the point, this she liked.
Sarah do half body massage, he was holding a lot of tension in his shoulders and thoracic spine, and he would cook dinner. Although they would have to go to the bustling markets together, on the mopeds, to select the desired ingredients and share the tab. Sorted.
Sarah felt an unusual harmonious connection. Thought of her own boy back home and internal mother qualities surfacing, as all mothers do. Ask their annoyed girlfriends!
Plus, his mum was the same age, so a great basis for a genuine platonic friendship. Steeped in Motherly love. Did Sarah miss her boy? Probably, yes.

She thought that if her own boy was found in the same situation, that she would hope that a kind, respectful lady would do the same and take of him under her wing? Beautiful karmic cycle relationships and all.

The morning rain awoke Sarah from her very deep sleep, she could hear the pitter patter as it sloshed outside off the gutters. This was the monsoon season, and it felt irresistibly rude not to go outside for a naked rain dance and a little splash about in the puddles with the lavender soap. Why not?

Her guest arrived mid-morning for his therapy treatment and Sarah lay her white bedding on the floor, then proceeded with her ritual to create the right ambiance. At times, following the visual guidelines from the Ancient Art of Thai Yoga Massage handbook given, and glancing at the picture cues as it lay spread out open on the floor.

It had been a few days since she had worked with the ham strings and the sophisticated folding of the lower legs and ankles maneuver. One has to be careful manipulating these areas in case of over application. Mo like to keep in shape with a specific physical training programme, so it was important not to aggravate any former problem areas. Sarah was a mindful bunny.

And it paid off too, as later that evening, Mo cooked the most delicious concoction of vegetarian savouries one could possibly imagine on a single gas ring. From Tantra with love. A plate of art and colour, combining punchy Moroccan and French influences akin.

Mo talked about his passion for truth and his love of Islam and cooking. What a blessing he brought to the table. Nourishing soulfood, which not only pleased the eye but confirmed what fundamental beliefs do to us all. Stripping down the walls of seeming separation from who we really are.

There was no denying it. Sarah had to go back home with Gratitude. Mo had helped with that decision too. Bless.

Sarah SpongeBob Squarepants sponge brain, learnt more about Islam over the subsequent days to follow, before deciding to leave and not extended the beautiful welcome that she had received on the very lovely, magical isle of Koh Phanghan.

Islam has a very beautiful message. Mohammed, peace be upon him, the prophet was a mortal man just like Jesus, Krishna and a whole host of other enlightened beings to name but a few. All conveying the same same message, just in various disguises, costumes, texts, word et al. Certainly not one being in it for the riches or Golden Glitter. Sarah was feeling this sentiment time and time again.

Mo was very concerned about the jinn on the island. His work, his passion his commitment and the lack of Muslim community, even though he sourced a dilapidated but interesting beautiful Mosque on the island, obscured from the road and neatly, tucked away under some over grown, jungle foliage.

The onslaught of another up and coming half moon party, played on his mind too. The drum roll and evening mantra beats, summoning the jinn to party and gather on the beaches. The disturbances of the dogs which increased, with each Moon party, as they chased island hopping revelers who bombarded the island, barking and snapping at their heels as they passed in vehicles, disgruntled him too.

He spoke of how he experienced the darkening of the sky in the presence of some unsavoury mortals, during prayer and the lowering of a golden sunset. Of feeling unsettled by beings cursed with jinn who would stare at him in restaurants, further un settled his mind. Sarah should know, he made her leave dinner early one evening, just by the glare of a stoned guy, out of his head on mushrooms.

He would also flip down the toilet seat to keep the jinn in as he told Sarah tales of them messing with people's bowels, eating their poo and other defecating interferences. Nor did Sarah keep up her Hindu wearing frontage in his presence. In respect of his God, Allah.

Sarah knew her consciousness and didn't need the costume anyway. She had a greater level of compassionate understanding from her beautiful Indian submersion. If Sarah felt the desire to pray to Ganesh, to help overcome any obstacles, she would. Goddess Kali had shown Sarah her wild courage to face her shadow and light, had shown her beauty in the eye of destruction and in the centre of a storm. She had got so deep in her numb chest, from rich Hindu experience, that she was pushing it out to open the hearts deeper longing.

Sarah embraced all customs and traditions and respected each one wholly and fully for their service they provided. C'est la vie!

Armed with an improved awareness, Sarah decided to fly over to Dubai, she had friends there thriving in explosive redevelopment. Sarah thought it a good suggestion to flex her skills at the vast array of co-joined yoga and massage centres advertised Dubai online. The idea of 2 for the price of 1 massage, buy 1 get 1 free, hahaha. Fully resonated with her.

A quick stop flying visit in Bangkok, to witness the delights, a must. Sarah felt pleased. Aligned.
Did she feel the need to call her husband, inform him of her next move? Tell him of her plans, her experiences? How could she. The conversation would go like this:
"Oh hi honey, how are you? By the way darling, I am have surrendered to my God self."
The line would go dead.
Yeah, she knew how that chat would go down. Like a lead balloon.
Mo, swang by for evening dinner. He had enough of his job. He quit. We talked this over into the night and life asked Sarah if he could join her in travels to Bangkok. His funds were scarce and co-sharing expenses seemed a viable option.
Of course, true to her generous, soft nature she agreed.

The next few days were spent cleaning, packing and organizing further accommodation. Aptly Sarah found a place called 'The Universe Home' just on the outskirts of KhaoSan Road, one of the most famous streets in Bangkok. Mo was short of cash, so we opted for the cheapest proposition, single beds. It was only for a couple of nights and would be fun. Mo had plans to fulfil a dream in Saudi Arabia and visit his beloved Mecca.
This was a very respectful boy, brought up with impeccable manners and devotion to his Allah. What is not to trust?
Whilst in Bangkok, Mo insisted that Sarah wear a headscarf so as not to draw attention to herself. Fair play, to any observing being, Sarah could look like a mature floozy, un married and parading around provocatively with a young Muslim entrepreneur. Complete in white Thobe.
Fact being, we were just helping each other greatly.
The night before departure Sarah allowed him to stay over at her bungalow for easy transition.

Unexpectedly, the following morning, an early morning 6am cab arrived, beeping furiously outside. Mo looked over at Sarah in wonder, neither of us had booked it? Sarah did not have the intention of 'sneaking off' either without proper goodbyes and thank you to the wonderful beings one had met on this incredible Thai high flying journey.

Incredibly, our bags were already packed and lined at the door. Life in Sarah's eyes, Allah in Mo's eyes, had given us a rite of passage to leave there and then rather than waiting around for the mid morning ferry. Let's go then. They both agreed.

Sarah threw a handful of Thai Baht, down on the kitchen counter, so as to cover the 'electri, the electri.' Would never offend the kindly Thai host, ex policeman and all. Beautiful man really.

The ferry went smoothly, the flight went smoothly, the taxi ride to KhaoSan Road reasonably well too, although Mo was a tough haggler and wouldn't be swindled on taxi fare overpayment. One would like to add, typical of masculine energy, but will refrain.

Sadly, the colorful city of Bangkok revealed to Mo a more disturbing eccentric mix off Jinn. This was Jinn city to him. The lady boys, the Satanist glow of intoxicating lights, the alcohol, the drugs, the craziness, all alluded him.

It did feel very different to the softness of the island that we had just come from indeed. Must agree. Yet, Sarah rather liked the contrast, the hedonistic sense of duality. Without it how can one grasp comprehensiveness? Of anything?

Thankfully, after a short exploration. He found himself a much cherished and impressive Mosque down some windy, tiny little back streets. One could hear the call to prayer, clearly so from the apartment building. Very soothing, romantic and powerful thought Sarah.

On the first night however, Mo raced to the door in his underpants, a resident across the hallway seemed to be deeply howling like a wolf, steadily as the Call to Prayer vibrations, beautifully echoed through those crazy a.m. Bangkok streets.

Wolfman sounded like he was in pain. His agony was seeping through the apartments thin walls, felt it in the very core of my being. Intense stuff. Did he need a calming massage Sarah thought? Not at this sleepy hour. Plus, the vibrational atmosphere felt significantly lowered.

Mo muttered that this reaction was normal to one possessed by the jinn, it was the bodies response to purification. To cleanse itself of the evil residing within. Fascinating insight.

Hastily, Mo washed in the bathroom and prepared for prayer. Then slipped out, leaving a bemused Sarah in bed to sleep some more.

Was this some sort of outrageous movie that Sarah was in the realms of? She certainly felt like it.

The following morning a grumpy Mo, did not appreciate being questioned by the 'said' howling Wolfman, in the foyer, about his origin. Nor did 'said' Wolfman exchange his true cultural domain. Preferring to fabricate his true country of origin. Oddly, but not oddly.

That cheerful, bright and breezy morning, Sarah's intuitiveness decided to visit the mosque, after peaceful morning practice down by the river. Although culturally not allowed inside, felt more than happy to sit in the grounds for a short while, to contemplate and lounge in its beautiful energy, in the sunshine before heading off down a little quaint side street, to share a light mushroom broth with some delightful Muslim women. Serving free meals from a little old-fashioned hatch, a few strides away from this fine Mosques entrance gates. Unable to communicate through English language, their smiles and hand gestures spoke volumes. More than enough to fill the heart with joy.

Amongst the nattering's of these cheerful woman, Sarah started to feel that she had had enough of her globe trotting and wild experiences.

She had seen, witnessed and observed more than her fair share, in any lifetime. The journey felt close to expiry. Would she settle in Dubai and make her home in the Middle East? Her friends had done so successfully, why not give it a try? Was this life's desire? Or would she give in and cave to the husband? Knowing full well of his utter bewilderment at his wife's follies and unresolved issues that we shared as a unit.

She felt that she had done more than enough work on herself, well enough for the time being, enough to sedate a horse in fact.

Ah well, all is well. Time to settle and arrive in a new zone.

Sarah was happy to part ways with Mo and board the plane bound for Dubai.

Inshallah friend.

Dengue Fever in Dubai

First observation upon arrival, no sacred numbers flashing up from life, no angel signs, no nothing; no clues for Sarah to gather that she was on the right path, that she was aligned and on her true soul mission.

She noted too that the heat felt different, more dry, intense and in line with the desert environment that she had now subjected herself too. Her body felt rather numb. Did this wonderfully clean and crisp country fully resonate with her from the outset?

Upon arrival, all beings were helpful enough in pointing out directions for the toilets, train station, ticket office juice bar, Wi-Fi hotspots etc., etc. You know the usual things a jet set traveller needs to prioritize for co-ordination purposes on landing and arriving in a new country. Sarah also had to find an ATM to exchange yet more foreign currency, to get her head around, so as to get out and about.

Feeling rather tired and a little in awe of these cleanly scrubbed, peacock looking Arab men, freshly presented and clucking around in big, clucking clusters. Sarah felt a little intimidated and longed for a friendly, female face to share a smile and identify with.

Sarah had never been to the Middle East before and had not felt it's masculine power and presence. Complete with little shepherd's cane walking stick ensemble.

Sarah was very curious what they used them for? To keep their wives in check?

The dignified embrace of this country felt very advanced and a futuristic technologist's dream. Everything was fandangle to the highest.

A brief stop to a coffee house (well she did need her a.m. caffeine fix) and a little update from an Italian English speaking women, gave Sarah a few much needed tips on getting out and about in the country, but most importantly on boarding the imminent train and its do's and don'ts. Sarah was so glad of the information so that she could respect this new countries values that she had just immersed herself into.

As she walked across the grand airport exit gates, out into the area to catch a connecting train, she couldn't help thinking what on earth was she doing here? Did she really feel like this was the place for her to share and develop her yoga and massage skills? Was she blindly deceived by the promise of wealth and success from the good old world web web's pictures and suggestions? Had her friends' constant flux of 'happy' Facebook photos, suggested to her that she was missing out on so much fun in the sun all year round? That Blighty was a rat race and Sarah was drowning in the rat soup and her soul so needed a change, a chance to evolve? That this majestic city of Dubai, held the magic key to Sarah's answers? She was going to find out for herself through direct experience. As ever. Tough, crazy cookie.

Sarah bought her train ticket from a pristine office, from a pristine ticket sales rep and walked along a pristine train platform, jumped in several pristine steel lifts to catch a most beautiful and elongated pristine train.

She remembered the Italian lady's words as she lugged her stuff and placed it in between her legs in the train's compartment. Do not eat, chew or place any rubbish on the floor. This faces a fine in this country and there are many community police officers patrolling about to ensure this beautiful city keeps it cleanliness reputation and high standards.

What she forgot to mention was not to sit in middle of the train as one would get harassed by local immigrants, up close and personal, challenging the comfort zone of proximity. A reserve cabin for woman travelers was at the back of the train. A big, Bart Simpson DOH! Ah well, Sarah wasn't harmed, she was used to Indian men from her experience anyway, and this close contact did not bother her in the slightest. It rather amused her actually.

Destination Sports City, here one comes. What one wasn't expecting was the heat to almost rip the eyelashes off the face as the doors folded back with a swish.

Fecking hell, 'its getting hot in here so take off all your clothes, I am getting so hot I wanna take my clothes off,' lyrics sprang to mind.

Just walking simple little baby steps to find a cab to the new crib was proving impossible, like walking through treacle with moonboots on.

What was wrong with the body. Sarah was adequately clothed for the environment and had consumed enough water so it wasn't from lack of hydration.

In Thailand, the body felt amazingly well, light, fresh, happy, alive. Something was wrong. Really wrong.

A few minutes later, she arrived at a really tall high rise block of flats, looking up into the skyline they seemed to go on forever. The full glare of the afternoon sun obscuring the eyes. Despite this, she could still observe the cranes and tarp covering partially built high rise flats that seemed to spring up all around, like some sort of futuristic, grandiose space station. One could hear the constant stammering of heavy drills, machinery and plenty of masculine energy hard at work; wonderfully constructing and co-creating such an impressive space, out there in the middle of the desert when once it had been just that, a barrage of sand. Amazing practical skills us humans have to use to create. Least we forget.

Sarah called the mobile number of her host and informed him of her immediate arrival. Room????? 7th floor up, here I come.

Sarah knocked on the door twice, her host knew of her arrival? Feelings of panic started to creep in.

After the 3ʳᵈ knock 2 very sleepy, muscular males appeared from behind the door. Oh shit, she thought for a minute. Sarah believed that she had booked the apartment for herself for the stay. Mistakenly, she hadn't checked the details on her App properly, what an airhead. The dope had rented a room and would be sharing with these 2 Turkish Muslims. How very nice.

However, the room was very light and airy and the host was definitely a professional and not a murderer. See how Doris has conditioned me?

The bed was nice and firm too.

Her 2 new flat mates gave her a short tour of the apartment block, there was a nice rooftop small swimming pool and plenty of open space for self practice.

Although, in this heat and from peering builder's eyes, maybe Happy Baby pose would be given a miss, it might give cause for some unnecessary tea breaks for the cheering workers across the way.

The gym was self contained and consisted of enough equipment to keep any gym junkie's physical energy moving adequately.

Plus, the Sports City was literally just across the road, so potential for work a huge winner, winner chicken dinner. Life, thank you this will do nicely.

Feeling relaxed and refreshed after a lovely, powerful, hot shower, the hosts took Sarah for a short ride to the Mall to pick up groceries in a most impressive shiny black, 4-wheel drive Land rover, complete with leather seats and full hit specifications. Sarah didn't know what they all where but knew that there were many interesting working gadgets right there in that beasty machine. Probably had an ejection seat build into it too like a James Bond mobile and could talk like Kit, the Knight-rider car. Take your pick, luxury boys toys are meant for playing with.

This was certainly a rather different form of transport and experience than the flip-flop wearing, scooter riding, Bedouin days spent mulling around the markets and back streets of the tropical jungle delights of Far East.

The shopping experience was also an eye opening experience. Row after row of delicious, organic, well presented combination of fruit and vegetables, full of life and multi nutritious vitamins kept alive with fresh mists of clean spray.

Usually, when Sarah goes shopping she gets excited by what ingredients she will put together and would fill up her trolley excitedly. However, she was feeling incredibly tired and worn out, just placing one foot in front of the other seemed to be a really conscious big effort that took the Monkey Mind off shopping or eating. What was going on internally?

She also felt like she was going to vomit. Oh dear. She didn't want to upset her hosts but had to ask them to cut short the shopping trip, even though they were filling up on BBQ beers and other things for a much needed chillax day out at the beach. The beach in this heat, it was by now at least 40 degrees baking hot. Sarah couldn't stand it any longer and insisted on going home to lie down. Which thankfully she did for the next 14 hours, until her consciousness was disturbed back into being by a ping notification email on her Ipad.

She leant over the bed to check it. Oh no, it was from her friend, dear Mo; he had been refused entry into Saudi, to go to his beloved Mecca. In a nutshell, in complete excitement he had forgot to check the visa requirements, of which he had none. Surprisingly, with little extra money, enough only to spare for few bottles of water along the way, and with Allah's help, he had persuaded the airline to change his ticket to Dubai. He was on his way and wanted to apartment share for a few days as he had secured an interesting job opportunity in nearby Abu Dhabi.

Oh well, he had asked for my help. What Mother could refuse. He was stuck, why not, there was another room available so Sarah pulled herself out of bed and asked the host if this was ok. No problem. These guys were not fazed, very accommodating in fact and then offered Sarah some Turkish tea and an interesting eggy dish combination? Sarah declined feeling queasy, she gave Mo the address then went back to bed fearing a temperature and heat motionlessness.

Within a few hours, there was a loud knock and a tired, pale, thin Mo stood at the door, bogged down by his rucksack and bags, ravenous by lack of food for several hours and weary by emotion. Sarah gave him a feeble hug and introduced him to her hosts. Being Muslim, they both got on like a house on fire although Turkish Muslim seemed to be more gentle and 'softer' than Mo's interpretation. Both equally beautiful in their own way. Complementing each others views as they rattled around in the kitchen preparing yet more food that Sarah could just not stomach and so she went back to bed. Fondly, listening to them prattling on about which news programme covered the most truth…Aljazeera? Was this closer to reality than the gunk churned out by the laxatives at the BBC? Force fed to millions? Who knew? It depended on the reality one lived in one supposed, she remembers thinking unclearly at the time.

And for the next 6 days she did not move from that pit. Funnily, nor did Mo from his. Through the walls she could here his moans, groans and deep sighs. Dear readers, this was not a case of man-flu either. As one might suspect. This illness was a completely debilitating one, it poleaxed one right out the body and mind.

The host pretty much left us to ourselves, although from time to time he politely knocked on each door to check that all was well and that both his guests were still breathing. Just about. Sarah googled the symptoms and checked in with the online doctor. Both Mo and Sarah had bizarrely contracted a severe bout of Dengue fever, both experiencing the same same malaria symptoms that had manifest at exactly the same time! That incidentally and synchronistically had sprung up from a lovely little insect bite in over in Thailand. When exactly, unsure of. Superb.

As the days unfolded the host suggested hospitalization, the blood count was dropping fast, an iv drip was possibly needed? Sarah's already tiny frame was shrinking even further. After a brief bathroom visit and run in the corridor, Sarah noted that Mo looked emaciated too. So much for his dream also. What would his mother think?

However, emergency treatment is only vital if the gums bleed too, good old WebDoctor confirmed, which Sarah stared at through slit eyes and immediately felt a surge of hope.

Sarah stayed put in bed, that was all that she could do. Suffering the cold, the cramps, the hallucinating, the delusions, the inability to swallow properly and she was rolling around in her own toxic smell, which was exuding out of her. So much so, for her new venture in Dubai. To experience no joys of a 2 hand massage or yoga. Bum cheeks.

Life was definitely indicating a big fat NO to this latest recklessness and the only way to listen to this misalignment was to lay the bugger up, sick as a dog and Mo too. Healing and suffering together as oneness.

Under a hazy spell of sheer desperation to desperately feel better, Sarah dragged herself out her flea infested pit and made her way up onto the rooftop for some much needed fresh air, the air con felt just too cold on the body which gave it more shivers. The 16 floor solo ascent seemed to go on forever and was just limitless.

As she weakly tried to open the heavy fire doors with limp wrists that held no strength, instead using the side hip to press against the opening and lever it open.

Woosh, the impact of the high heat sucked her outside like the opening of a hot oven door, Sarah felt cooked. There was no chance of self practice either, it was just too hot and she was still too weak.

The energy she used just to get there was already over expended and she needed to sit and rest awhile. Gingerly, she climbed up to the roof top barrier walls and dangled her legs over the sides. Flicking her feet in the winds, feeling at one with the clouds, quiet and still, no one to talk to, no one to needily grasp one's attention.

Sarah looked down and noticed the tiny little ants scurrying about their business in the car park below. She didn't realize just how high up she was. Nor how low she was feeling. In one split instant she felt the urge to literally slip off and disappear for good. To get rid of the body and its constant nattering once and for all.

Sarah doesn't know how long passed, but it was probably a while, as she sat there contemplating. No-one would know if it was an accident or intentional. One could just slip right on over the edge. Plus, the pavement below looked rather inviting from this view, perched high in the sky like an eagle ready to soar.

Somewhere deep within, brought Sarah's attention to the time, she glanced at her watch, her Dad's Omega watch. Something within registered what had she been doing, she was not aligned with source. What's more, a poor kid had followed her over here as well? Get a grip you crazy woman, is this what your awakening has come to?

Sarah returned to her senses and dragged her feet once more over the ledge, got back into the lift, descended down to the confines of her friendly hosts and sick companion.

With a renewed sense of vigor, she knew what to do. She crawled into bed, under the covers as the air con was just too cold, then booked her flight back to the UK whilst writing a letter of apology to her hubby, informing him of her imminent return home. That all was not well and that she had been very sick. Lack of insurance kept her away from hospital treatment but with the help of life and natural healing, she had managed to sweat it out. Sarah would manage the flight home, as her condition was improving daily, and that she was sorry but not sorry, for leaving without a full heart to heart. Could she be forgiven and be allowed back into the family home? After all, half was legally hers and she so wanted to face the music with her kids and settle things straight once and for all.

In her gut, she felt as though her tail was caught between her legs. She knew, deep down, that the family would consider that she had abandoned them. Who could blame them.

However, Sarah was caught in a very different paradigm though now. Life had suggested a return home, for Karmic Housekeeping as the cure.

This was her alignment for sure.

Before leaving, it was so needed to sample the delights of this creative, juicy city lurking outwards and upwards from this giant illuminated sandpit. A city with real forward thinking pleasures to behold.

Sarah took a few days to wander round slowly, had started to nibble on little bites too. She had to explore the famous Jumeirah beach and dip one's toes in the sea, alongside a vast wide range of multi dimensional other beings, who thoroughly enjoyed the coolness of the water.

Not to forget to mention either, the joys to be able to walk along the quay side in admiration of the fabulous range of expensive sports cars lined up out there and observe boat loads of party boat revelers, playing beats, swigging champagne, dressed in Dior bikinis and matching designer tattoos sleeves. Incredible to witness. A big, fat Wow. If you're into that sort of thing.

This was an unconceivable dream to observe, yet sadly not one for Sarah. She felt more like a pig in shit in her beloved Far East, whose humbler, frugal nature really inspired her to BE. That said. It is always a good opportunity to experience contrast. Plus, Sarah had been very, very, poorly for a while which definitely lowered her vibration.

Mo on the other hand, had a more important mission to complete and spent the days selling himself, very successfully too, in this land of many promises. We sealed our goodbyes with a nice hug.

Sarah packed her up her things, for the last time in a long while she hoped, and made way to the airport with a lift in her generous host's swanky black, land rover. Silently purring like a jaguar, cruising the desolate streets in the dead, still desolate early morning highway. Sarah knew this was the right thing to do and swallowed a few Aspirin just to be on the safe side. Bear in mind this yogi had not touched any prescription drugs for over a year now, this was a very radical thing for her to do. She WOULD get on that plane in the morning by hook or by crook! And minus a temperature for sure!

Weak and exhausted but happy to be returning home to see what life had in store. Sarah did not recall any of the journey home as she slept most of the way. The bout of Dengue fever had certainly left an imprint in her blood cells. Going without self practice even for a day was frowned upon by her, let alone a week. She knew too that she had been totally blessed to be able to catch a flight back to Manchester at such short notice, as and when she did.
Inshallah.

Karmic Housekeeping

So I found myself standing alone, once more, on the grey pavements of a very grey English airport terminal car park. Aptly feeling grey too.

Sensitive to the the nip in the air, I took a spare, wooly sweater and scarf out my hand luggage, put them on and glimpsed at my reflection in the huge glass panels as I zipped up my puffa jacket as well.

Blimey, I had shrunk; my clothes were literally hanging off me. I had shriveled to a puny 47kg, which was certainly on the low size for me. An ideal weight of a 10-year old maybe, but not to a lady of my years. Fast approaching half a century.

Quickly, I rang the husband on the mobile to let him know that I had safely arrived and of my whereabouts. In error and in a total blind panic and frantic state, he had driven to the wrong terminal. He was approximately 10 minutes away.

"Stay put," he ordered.

I only had to wait a few short minutes before I saw him, anxiously striding towards me. I could feel his nervous energy approaching before he did.

Thoughtful as ever, despite our lack of communication and connection, he had hurriedly parked the car in a nearby bay so that he could help carry the bags. Always a gentleman.

As I got in the passenger seat, I took a long side glance at his profile. What had I put this man through? Or should I reframe that, what had this dear man put himself though in my absence?

I noticed that he had gained quiet a few extra white hairs in his beard, a few extra facial lines, a thinner parting and thicker midriff. Despite all of the obvious signs of anxiety, I could still feel the love in his heart, he had just been suffering ego rejection that's all.

However, on the short car ride home I felt unable to apologize for my actions or seemingly reckless behavior.

I could sense that he had many questions which I could not answer in a moving vehicle and nor without eye contact. I could feel the emotion of rage filling up inside of him.

Nor could I tell him about my experiences in any brief detail. Where to start?

Silence is more appropriate sometimes.

On arriving at the family home, I immediately felt like a cat on a hot tin roof.

Unable to settle and feeling full of remorse. It was obvious that I had uncovered some long forgotten dark shadows, that still needed healing. For the sake of us all.

Hence life frog marching me home, to work through these little buggers.

Even if it meant feeling like shit, vomit and death all rolled into one. Indeed, my path had taken me a few too many steps backwards and gone full circle, right back to the beginning of time. Confused? I am too.

Ram Dass says, '*Suffering is a form of grace.*'

For apparent reasons, Sarah and I had to go through this process, for the self and the family. In order to mind sweep this karmic housekeeping once and for all. Life demanded it.

The self suggested that I had to work through these emotions, whilst wearing my new guise. I had become a different player and had certainly let go of the beliefs that didn't serve me anymore. This next part of my story would for sure uncover what else needed to be examined, allowed, acknowledged and released.

As a family, we certainly had a lot of speaking to do, all round. From the deep and loving, open arms of the heart space.

My beautiful kids thought that I had abandoned them, and naturally questioned their Father as to why I was allowed back in the house?

Nor would they be prepared to accept my full apology or allow me to slip back into the role as Chief dumper driver that easily, they both confirmed.

Oh well so be it, I would have to be seen to be suffering as they did. Really, who could blame them either. This was their reality.

Fact is, I never abandoned them, I never would. I am their Mother. I always will be. My love for them is of ascension caliber, limitless and beyond timelessness.

Every minute of every day, they are a constant in my heart and I continually send them tons of love and beautiful wishes. To all my friends and family members and people that I don't even know too. To squished road stew on the ground that I might come across on a bike ride, to homes needing love, to my food, my bed, my laptop and for the space in between which connects 'it' all, giving everything a sense of purpose. Guess the list is endless. My days are certainly kept busy! So many blessing and thoughts of gratitude are constantly sent out. It's a bit like being a modern day Mrs. Santa Claus! Tons of fun!

Currently, my kids are not aware yet of the many models of motherly love or stability that co-exist. They let the old belief system get in the way and their expectations come under a false premise of how a parent should be. How would they possibly know any different either? I had part-provided the programming for their own internal conditioning from my own former pre-fear model of reality.

Little did they realize that my 12-month journey of self, of adventure and healing, would in fact benefit them tremendously. If they opened their closed hearts to it.

On the 1st evening, I made myself a little sacred shrine with candles in the study, shut the door tightly, pulled out a sleeping bag and sobbed my eyes out. I didn't have the inclination or the desire to sit with the stillness of simply being in meditation. The pain that was coming up was just too intense. It had to be released. It was healing in modality. I had to tenderly hold this inner child's grief securely. Honor it and treasure it, for as long as it took to pass.

That night, through tear stained cheeks, I slept on the floor in self punishment. Even though we had plenty of spare comfortable beds. Before bed, I didn't even take off my puffa jacket, change out of my travelling clothes or brush my teeth. That would spend too much energy.

Even declining the caring hubby, when he generously offered me his bed to sleep in too.

No, Sarah and I wanted to feel this pain. It was a significant expression of healing and even the kids had set this vortex of emotion into play. A shift was evident for change to take place, my energy was different, my beliefs were too. I had a different model of expansion which was no coincidence as it came through my authentic, nothing self.

Unsettling as it may be.

Over the next few days, we talked over coffee as the regular routines of before rolled on.

The hubby and I needed some space, the teenage energy monsters agreed and temporarily moved out to spend a spell with their respective partners. Well, they spent much of the time at their places anyways. This was no big deal.

A plan of action was needed to create a safe space for intimacy, for trust and for love to be revealed. To determine, whether or not our hearts had fully separated or that full closure of the relationship, in the marital sense anyway, held the answer.

Sadly, and all to frequently, we hear that a marriage ends when 1 person 'falls out of love' with another. What does that mean? I can only assume that the butterflies have escaped the belly and that the physical attraction that was once there, has had the lights dimmed. That the love vibration no longer gives off overwhelmingly, pulsating frequencies. And that the hearts, which were once so close that only need whisper to each other, were now that far apart that they had to shout over each other to be heard.

We are so conditioned to believe that we can measure love, that there is a right way to love, or that you can give an adequate quantity of love, which signals that you're with the right partner. Correct?

Just as there are many healthy ways to have a fulfilling, enriching partnership; I have already mentioned there are many ways to tantric love, 'Tan,' to expand, 'tra,' the tool. There are numerous ways to say, 'I love you,' and express this with your partner.

There is an appreciation you feel when they do something thoughtful and kind, like remember your birthday or take the rubbish out to the bin without asking. The room literally glows in their presence and dims when they leave. You feel tingly inside when they kiss you. You feel gratitude to be present with them and know they feel the same about you. The deep, mutual trust you feel does not falter when 'problems' come up, in fact it deepens it.

Likewise, there are so many other ways to love when we tune our awareness and widen our consciousness to include these variations, default by our very narrow cultural definition. It's infinitely richer than the images portrayed on the big screens, infinitely more alive than the 1-dimensional feeling of butterflies that sometimes initiates a relationship.

It's appreciation, comfort, joy, gratitude, warmth, tingles, trust, awe, softness, real, honest and raw too.

So did I feel these toward the hubby?

One lunchtime, as I sat sipping a green smoothie, I came across a Facebook post from Neale Donald Walsch. It read:

'Words may help you understand something, but experience allows you to know. Never trade your own experience for someone else's words about anything that is really important. Like God or love or what is true about another.'

And we did. We allowed the weeks to unfold, graciously and tenderly to see what came up.

In due course and with the greatest respect, it was clearly evident that our hearts and paths were not serving us alchemically as nature intended. Specifically, not benefitting each other as one was co-existing within separate dimensions and levels of consciousness awareness.

The storm would not blow over. The karmic or conditioned fear driven by every self centred decision that was ever made needed to be burnt up, it would not go away. The hubby and I had to sit right in the middle of the storm and feel the winds.

We were afraid of ourselves, perhaps due to having parents who were similarly afraid of themselves. We had established a perfectly functional co-dependent relationship up until recent years. Although both of us hadn't accepted our God given gifts or shadows.

I had given up on the approach to life to feed the one time, companion and friend, Monkey Mind. The Monkey Mind was mischievous, bouncing around from place to place, messing with everything. But as I learnt from sitting on my meditation cushion, he wasn't so cute. Just like my Dad had warned me on his death bed in hospital.

"Watch out for them damn spider monkeys, they are everywhere!" He lovingly claimed.

That is exactly what Monkey Mind is like. In reality, he is not a pet, he is wild, vicious and unpredictable.

One cannot squeeze his cheeks and say he's cute. You want to run like hell and hide in your expectations, memories, regrets and ideas. Most times, Sarah felt like she was running through the jungle with her tail on fire. That she did, as you know.

One evening, over a beautiful dinner in a swanky restaurant whilst discussing all things financial with the hubby, I recalled a song blaring out through the speakers, Monkey Mind's favourite: You help me lose my Mind, by London Grammar. I vividly recollect the sadness filling up inside, and the sudden loss of appetite as the chorus kicked in. I certainly couldn't finish stuffing the Pear Tarte Tatin and vanilla cream down my throat. It felt like swallowing lead. Not like I would do that of course! Nor encourage little ones to do that even!

The hubby, bless him, didn't have a clue what was going on internally. He just politely paid the bill and then we left so that he could fall asleep, in his favourite, comfy chair.

It was an amicable, mutual decision to part ways, to dissolve the energetical ties that forced us to be unhappily together.

The marriage had been killed by lack of respect. When that kicks in and you start putting yourself down, to make yourself smaller, well that is a fatal line to cross. Also, I had lived in the masculine energy for way too long. The system downshift into this new feminine energy was a surprisingly tall order for the hubby to digest on many levels.

The financial tiding up shortly followed; to sell the house and end the marriage securely. We had been so blessed to enjoy the years we did. Wow, what an honor to share all those years with such a fabulous, incredible guy and to have co-created the most amazing and talented kids too. Circumstances certainly do not make a man, they reveal him.

Thanks to life. We are always and in all ways blessed.

Amen.

Enquiry within Nature: Scottish Buddhist Retreat

So what next? No next...I felt the desire for contrast, for quiet and solitude and the need to absorb plenty of green, leafy, hearty nature. The rugged variety. The George Clooney kind. ;-)

Of late, I had spent so many wonderful moments basking in the lush tropical golden climates of the Far East and experiencing the intense humidity of the Middle, that my body was craving hardy elements. The wind, the rain and the cold. In particular, lots and lots of juicy mud to squelch through on desolate, off beaten tracks. The type that gets your running shoes soaked, right through to the muddy toenails, which is pure joy to clean up afterwards. To feel the swirling wind as it runs through the body, even wrapped in several thermal layers, as it descents a steep, weathered hill. No traffic to navigate only the fleeting eyes of curious sheep. To appreciate the soft folds of the windswept landscape, boldly radiating greens, oranges and brown textures as far as the eye could stretch, blending magically into the still iridescent silvery skyline. Bliss.

A fleeting search on the good, old interweb proposed a Buddhist Weekend Meditation Retreat in the rugged Scottish hills. Further research advised that the centre attracted, 'Thousands of visitors a year,' that visit to enjoy the magnificent temple and grounds, which self supports monks and nuns and their teachings of how to lead a compassionate life.

Another pleasing advantage was that an international best selling author was running the course. Her books had been translated in over 30 languages. She was a former special needs teacher, her writing reflected the stories encountered by emotionally damaged souls. Plus, the online course material made reference to her own internal dialogue about meditation from a Western perspective with suggestions of how to develop a sound meditation practice.
This was all the information I needed to engage. Those beautiful words jumped out from the webpage and resonated deeply in the heart space.
Quick as one can say, 'Jack Rabbit,' the diminishing credit card was whipped out to secure a place immediately. There is no time like the present!

Of course, the peace and tranquility was second to none. The nourishment amazing. The refreshment for stillness and silence within, supreme. The sharing of this wonderful being's wisdom through her very loving presence, I held dearly within my heart. Further consolidating the internal belief that love in not a form of something but a field, something that we cannot get but are. Nothing but love. Compassionate Metta.

Under a midnight blue sea of twinkling stars, it became clear that my vehicle of consciousness, in all its majestic forms, was evolving daily. Sarah and I had embodied simplicity, out of being in the depths of complexity.

Coming Home with Gratitude to a place of inner peace was born out of one's hard graft of self and jottings; scribbled down in that very blank A4 notepad I bought at the start. In which I religiously carried around with me for the last 12 crazy, head-the-ball (Dads pet name for me) months. While I feel that the only 'real' religion, consists in having a good heart, just as the Dalai Lama says.

Coming Home with Gratitude

Dear ones, here we are.
Finally, safely arriving together at the closing chapter, aptly titled don't you think? Who thinks? Lol.
What an incredibly blessed 12-month journey of adventure and healing one has had.

Did you enjoy drinking it up?
My very own enlightened non-alcoholic cocktail of knowledge about life and death. However, it is only my interpretation, rather than the objective truth, please remain aware.

How is Sarah feeling now? Consciousness? Expansion? Oneness?
Well for starters oozing lots and lots of juicy love from a big, fat, juicy, open, spiritual heart, as I currently rest in a very beautiful, sumptuously decorated rental home.
Feeling very blessed to be nestled in the North of Portugal, in a secluded little village on the outskirts of my beloved nature and wildlife.
Additionally, the masculine sun is shining very brightly and sending lots of healing energetic vibrations through the entrance door, across the table and enveloping my petite feminine with a nice, juicy cuddle as I type away fluidly. The conditions are just perfect to stimulate the creative juices and conclude this final chapter of my story and intense 12-month awakening to self. Feeling as though I have not been writing this book at all, but in truth, that it has been in fact writing me.

The result of which, has taken me across many continents, thrown me in many exhilarating and obscure situations, both offering light and dark dualistic contrasts, akin to the love story of Romeo and Juliet. The mission? To confront and nurture the inner child, the dark shadows and gripping ego aka the grasping Monkey Mind. Who incidentally, is a very good, quiet boy these days! Thanking too, all the BEings who lit my path along the way and continually do so. More love.
Blessed to be pouring such unreserved loving energy into the final chapters of, my story thus far, for the time BEing. Some more love, love, juicy love.

Unable to speak the lingo but gladly receiving a wealth of tasty treats such as, fresh oranges and lemons complete with cute storks, hand picked from the neighbours trees and thick slices of homemade cake and freshly baked bread, in passing, to my very grateful, open hands. I feel that the generous big hearted locals are feeding my passion and simultaneously supporting my moral. I couldn't feel any happier.

This majestic life has beautifully given me everything my heart could desire, to allow this natural gracious sharing to unfold and a to do what next with? Life knows, but not I for now. I am still in the slip stream of abundance, simply allowing the unfolding without resistance.

Happy to take daily walks, to invigorate the physical body, stretch the legs and meander down the hill, to a local street tabac, for a decadent chai tea. Unable to converse with the residents but content to remain silent and with pure source.

Happy to observe and witness delightful exchanges that go on. As and when they do.

Happy to continue my self practice in the local square, much to the amusement of the old dears, who question…

"Gymnastica? Gymnastica?"

"Non, Yoga," replied another.

This I can make translate.

Happy to cycle to the local market to buy fresh fruit and vegetables for nourishing, loving soups and smoothies.

Happy to bathe, sing and dance along with Madonna, playing my favourite song, Vogue and to strike some naked poses in a sparkly, jewel encrusted bathroom mirror during my morning ritual. Thanking each perfect body part in turn, as I massage the coconut oil in, for working so well and supporting me. Even after seizing up a little through sitting for hours at an end, typing away energetically on my beautiful Mac notebook, lovingly sharing with you all that wants to be shared.

Happy to keep my fingers warm, by dangling them over fragranced lit candles when they start to feel rather cold and numb. Even though cold and numb are my friends now too.

Plus, feeling mega happy with the gift of high speed internet connection, so that I can verbally communicate, as and when needed, with all my loved ones and partners in co-creation.

Furthermore, I feel very happy and full of gratitude to my latest new connection. A real life Portuguese Angel, whose passion for creativity is very similar to mine but just has a different expression, Art. Her paintings arouse such provocative, passionate feelings within me. Witnessed via their presence alone, after a private viewing in a humble and homely well lit apartment, set high in the atmosphere of a tumbling, luminous Lisboan skyline.

The collection took my breath away. I momentarily found myself lost in the infinite life. Nor, did I notice that I had accidentally leant on one of her most recent expressions. A gift for a small child, very cleverly painted with a secret neon iridescent glow. What a clumsy me! Beautifully, she sourced an immediate solution.

Obrigada lovely soul.

What else had I learnt?

I had conquered the non-attachment to my desired outcomes of mind and its thoughts, my body, my breath, with people or this story book even.

I had come to feel and to know that I was an infinite soul on an infinite journey through life and to feel the peace or silence inside. Living in this body as a multi dimensional and singular human being. Moving through the life as motion, as motion is the nature of this majestic life, remember? No thing is not moving. Allowing life to flow through me and not simply happening to me.

In other words, I had learnt to let go of my life, of going beyond the ego, living as the soul and feeling completely happy with it as it is now, and now and now and now and now and now and now and now and now....And what a transformation from such a closed, controlling feminine Alpha, Shiva of yesteryear!

Moreover, I found through letting go and trusting the process, of that which no longer served me, Sarah found…Freedom and love for what and who I already was and in turn, this allowed me to let go in my heart of hearts and I totally surrendered and lost interest in the outcome. The kundalini energy too. I was spent trying to control it, I just let it pass through. For example, by going off by myself for a naked swim in the ocean, to scream out loud if need be and let the energies flow. Surrendering to the bliss of the divine and the aliveness in my body and sense of presence.

As a result ?

I soon realized that the perfect outcomes always manifested anyway. This beloved life of ours does not make mistakes. It creates the most beneficial experience for your soul's evolution, providing one with the opportunity to re-create one's life as one fully wants it to be.

Needless to say, what did I do?

I became a fully fledged student of love and gathered a stack of resources to create an emotional tool kit for self care service. Bit like a construction worker utilizing a tool kit full of essential equipment. Only mine was full of loving self help strategies and anecdotes.

Firstly, I began writing a self care list of all the things that I would accept in my life:
Tantric love, freedom, honesty, support, tenderness, truth, new experiences, evolution, silence and nature. I wrote a list of what I would not too, essentially the opposite.
Additionally, take note, I knew that I had to practice these partnership skills daily, and that it was a decision to love with intention on a soul hook level which would provide optimal healing on the deepest parallel, drawing the right vibe to attract the tribe and so forth. I also knew that everyone shows love differently, acts of love and service are varied, some like roses and gifts, others don't care.

How do I do this on a practical level?

By adopting a similar principle from educational know-how from taught PE lessons and transmitting them through a successful holistic sense via a Traffic Light system that I devised. Fondly aware of how kids used to love playing this particular game with me in school. ☺

Red:
Stop ask yourself questions on a daily basis. What kind of thoughts are going through the mind all day long? Are they kind? Are they right? Are they good for me? Good for others? Are they good questions for our beloved Mother Earth?
Handy Hint:
If a few negative ones crop up, forgive them then allow them to pass. Understanding that the viral infection of the mind will subside as it can lead to enormous self inflicted suffering. I learnt to observe and pay full attention to the thoughts in my head. Thus creating 2-dimensions in my mind; the thoughts and the awareness.
The being in the grip of the ego Monkey Mind is so identified with the thoughts that there is no awareness. That state which generates suffering.
Going off on a tangent but sometimes this suffering operates on a collective level. As we know and are aware of the conflicts between the Sunni and Shite Muslims. Both are Muslims but in disagreement about something that happened hundreds of years ago. This is how the ego Monkey Mind cunningly operates. He causes separation, conflict and violence. That which we are not.

Green:
Trust in the process that you have the green light and put the pedal to the metal-full throttle. Go, go, go!

Amber:
Focus and be fully alert in day to day pauses. Inevitably this will lead you to become more conscious of people you meet, more grateful to them and as to why they crossed your path?

Black:
Black? I hear you question? Just like my bemused kids used to do in school to, standing there frozen, rooted to the giant floor of the PE Hall in wonder? What does this verbal instruction challenge?

Black, yes black, Miss Black knows there is black, it is imperious. Without the black plastic frame of a traffic light unit, there would be no bulbs, no colour and certainly no instruction or order.

Black is acceptance. To learn it in the here and now and recognize the necessity to bow to it. Sometimes, even now when unpleasant thoughts and feelings come up and don't and won't go away, I will sit with them and stay very present with them, even when they keep me from my beautiful sleep. This is perfectly ok too. They are not blocks or blockages either, just part of the present scene.

I learnt to fully breathe deeply and fuller into uncomfortable sensations, giving them dignity, honoring them instead of closing them off. On the in-breathe imagining the tenderness and neglected area of the body filling up on love and light. Like a little baby, they wanted to be held, met and honored in the present moment also. Coming to understand that even discomfort holds intelligence, that it is not against you. Waking up to the knowledge that true joy is not in the absence of joy or pain but in the willingness to embrace it all.

The breath, relaxation and presence awareness are essential ingredients of transformation too. Sometimes my 'I AM' presence just pops right out during Savasana, (Corpse pose, a favourite) or by a walk in the woods or bathing in the shower. One is constantly surprised.
Coming Home with Gratitude has seen me let go of what 'they' wanted me to be, reflecting that projected needy illusion out into a prescribed society.

I simply chose to merge back into God, the divine intelligence, consciousness, call it what you will. God is what you say God is. Truth is what you say truth is. Words and definitions are what one believes them to define. One gets my drift?
I also chose to surround myself with beings who had also escaped the illusion through grace too. How blessed I AM.

In choosing to invest in my sanity and shy away from this saturated, consumer based mind society. I now feel that I am on the right path of continuous growth and expansion, into the body and soul I was designed to live in. With it, a fresh, new sense of Sarah equilibrium, of integrity of becoming blossoms daily. Thanks to life!

So all is perfectly well, spring has nearly sprung and with it comes the promise of new life. Just in harmonious synchronization with the arrival of the dawn chorus and the days getting lighter and brighter. A perfect opportunity to re-create ourselves anew in the most magnificent version of ourselves that we can possibly imagine in this moment, just like nature does. Although winter is having her last say, and blast, for a little while longer yet I feel. Back in blighty for sure and even here in the warmer, sunnier climates of a cherished Portugal as well!

Always and never are lies too. Doris you never told me that as a kid growing up! Wink, wink! Sarah and I never use them anymore. There is only now, now and now your only place of TRUE POWER. A great intelligence is alive in us all. The power is to realize this and connect with the 'it' source.

Lastly, I had woken up from a million years of conditioning. Huge Cat/Cow yawn and leg stretch pose prompted here right now. Even though at times, I thought I was lost in the story/movie and felt totally disconnected.

Lao Tzu, a Buddhist teacher, quotes that,

'New beginning are often disguised as painful endings.'

So true. Sometimes on my path, I experienced the painful lesson first then the experience. Other times, the experience first and the lesson sunk in afterwards. I learnt to pay attention so that I didn't come up with the same mistake twice.

We are programmed to evolve through this mechanism because nature has been involved in the process of transmutation for 3.5 billion years, give or take a few years on earth. Once a teacher, always a teacher and all that jazz hands stuff. We just can't get enough of trivial facts. Love 'em in fact.

What is apparent now too is this:

Sarah feels ready to enter a co-creative relationship, which is truly alchemical. The cells of the body crave it. Why? Because God designed our bodies to be used in his glory. His glory as a spiritual act of worship. That it is not purely a physical union, but has a deep spiritual reality to it. As I have already mentioned, I feel the body and soul are not really 2 separate entities but intertwined with one another.

Sarah feels that she is ready for a team effort of dedication, in gratitude of who you are and what you want as being the point. Bathing together in a conscious relationship experiencing love as not the final destination, but as the fuel for the journey, simply 2 beings looking to express 100% themselves. United as a soul coupling that you feel physically and emotionally safe with.

My Alpha/Shiva male, the one that I will eventually attract, will form with me an infinite, strong, powerful and deep relationship and he's going to have it all. Strong, sensual, a giver and healer, healed and powerful, certain of his Godly presence. He knows that he is GOD himself and hence our dance together will flow in a beautiful wave of co-creation and full blown partnership. Loving happily ever after. How does that sound?

In the meantime, I will have enjoyed exploring the diversity and feeling the radiance in beings' eyes! I am a woman and I want to be a Blondie, continually expanding, having fun and enjoying to live. Honouring the not knowing, like a small emergent kid building sandcastles, knocking them down and then rebuilding them better each time they are smashed down. Resisting as well, muddy entanglement, favouring only clear entanglement as I will not leak my energy where it does not serve.

Finally paying Gratitude to my/our dearly loved beloved Father, whose passing from his physical body was the meaningful catalyst for my individual awakening.

Bless you and love you always. I will not die with my magic still within.

One has to embrace this sentiment as one starts getting older. As one matures, one naturally loses a lot of people, which makes one realize that each day is a gift one to be to be thankful for. Doesn't one lovely Doris darling?

Not only for the self but the souls of others too.

Wishing you boundless, juicy love and light.

Sending you more blessings with a poem that I scribbled down:

When I leave go inside the heart,

That's where I'll be.

No nature of time in this wondrous existence.

Feel and know this.

Contemplation is power.

Express Gratitude every day for that.

What's beautifully unfolding right now?

'Scarce are those with no train to catch'...

"Thank you for sharing Mooji Baba." My dear friend Monkey Mind inserts.

Om. Amen. Inshallah. Bless. Shanti. Shanti. Shanti.

Nothing but Love...No thing

Namaste...

Laters...

Made in the USA
Middletown, DE
15 April 2017